D1313753

1st EDITION

Perspectives on Modern World History

The Assassination of Martin Luther King, Jr.

1st EDITION

Perspectives on Modern World History

The Assassination of Martin Luther King, Jr.

Noah Berlatsky

Book Editor

GREENHAVEN PRESS
A part of Gale, Cengage Learning

GALE
CENGAGE Learning™

Detroit • New York • San Francisco • New Haven, Conn • Waterville, Maine • London

Christine Nasso, *Publisher*
Elizabeth Des Chenes, *Managing Editor*

© 2011 Greenhaven Press, a part of Gale, Cengage Learning.

Gale and Greenhaven Press are registered trademarks used herein under license.

For more information, contact:
Greenhaven Press
27500 Drake Rd.
Farmington Hills, MI 48331-3535
Or you can visit our Internet site at gale.cengage.com.

ALL RIGHTS RESERVED.
No part of this work covered by the copyright herein may be reproduced, transmitted, stored, or used in any form or by any means graphic, electronic, or mechanical, including but not limited to photocopying, recording, scanning, digitizing, taping, Web distribution, information networks, or information storage and retrieval systems, except as permitted under Section 107 or 108 of the 1976 United States Copyright Act, without the prior written permission of the publisher.

For product information and technology assistance, contact us at
Gale Customer Support, 1-800-877-4253.

For permission to use material from this text or product, submit all requests online at
www.cengage.com/permissions.

Further permissions questions can be e-mailed to permissionrequest@cengage.com.

Articles in Greenhaven Press anthologies are often edited for length to meet page requirements. In addition, original titles of these works are changed to clearly present the main thesis and to explicitly indicate the author's opinion. Every effort is made to ensure that Greenhaven Press accurately reflects the original intent of the authors. Every effort has been made to trace the owners of copyrighted material.

Cover image Custom Medical Stock Photo, Inc. Reproduced by permission.

LIBRARY OF CONGRESS CATALOGING-IN-PUBLICATION DATA

The assassination of Martin Luther King, Jr. / Noah Berlatsky, book editor.
    p. cm. -- (Perspectives on modern world history)
    Includes bibliographical references and index.
ISBN 978-0-7377-5259-5 (hardcover)
1. King, Martin Luther, Jr., 1929–1968--Assassination--Juvenile literature. I. Berlatsky, Noah.
    E185.97.K5A86 2011
    323.092--dc22
                                                                                    2010042117

Printed in the United States of America
1 2 3 4 5 6 7 15 14 13 12 11

CONTENTS

for justice and freedom. He says that even if he does not live a long life he is satisfied in knowing that the struggle will be successful.

CHAPTER 2   Controversies Surrounding the Assassination of Martin Luther King, Jr.

government agencies were involved in the assassination or in a cover-up.

A nonprofit foundation that researches controversial assassinations argues that there is much contradictory evidence around the murder of Martin Luther King, suggesting a conspiracy or a cover-up, perhaps even involving government officials. They suggest that all records pertaining to the case should be made public so that the truth can be investigated.

A Pulitzer Prize-winning author argues that James Earl Ray is a con artist who has fooled the King family and others into believing he is innocent of the assassination of Martin Luther King despite the solid evidence against him.

A historian says that President Lyndon Johnson used the sentiment and the riots following King's death as an occasion to push the Fair Housing Act through Congress, where it had stalled. The law guaranteed that blacks could not be discriminated against in purchasing homes.

FOREWORD

"History cannot give us a program for the future, but it can give us a fuller understanding of ourselves, and of our common humanity, so that we can better face the future."

—*Robert Penn Warren,*
American poet and novelist

The history of each nation is punctuated by momentous events that represent turning points for that nation, with an impact felt far beyond its borders. These events—displaying the full range of human capabilities, from violence, greed, and ignorance to heroism, courage, and strength—are nearly always complicated and multifaceted. Any student of history faces the challenge of grasping the many strands that constitute such world-changing events as wars, social movements, and environmental disasters. But understanding these significant historic events can be enhanced by exposure to a variety of perspectives, whether of people involved intimately or of ones observing from a distance of miles or years. Understanding can also be increased by learning about the controversies surrounding such events and exploring hot-button issues from multiple angles. Finally, true understanding of important historic events involves knowledge of the events' human impact—of the ways such events affected people in their everyday lives—all over the world.

Perspectives on Modern World History examines global historic events from the twentieth-century onward by presenting analysis and observation from numerous vantage points. Each volume offers high school, early college level, and general interest readers a the-

1

matically arranged anthology of previously published materials that address a major historical event, with an emphasis on international coverage. Each volume opens with background information on the event, then presents the controversies surrounding that event, and concludes with first-person narratives from people who lived through the event or were affected by it. By providing primary sources from the time of the event, as well as relevant commentary surrounding the event, this series can be used to inform debate, help develop critical thinking skills, increase global awareness, and enhance an understanding of international perspectives on history.

Material in each volume is selected from a diverse range of sources, including journals, magazines, newspapers, nonfiction books, personal narratives, speeches, congressional testimony, government documents, pamphlets, organization newsletters, and position papers. Articles taken from these sources are carefully edited and introduced to provide context and background. Each volume of Perspectives on Modern World History includes an array of views on events of global significance. Much of the material comes from international sources and from US sources that provide extensive international coverage.

Each volume in the Perspectives on Modern World History series also includes:

- A full-color **world map**, offering context and geographic perspective.
- An annotated **table of contents** that provides a brief summary of each essay in the volume.
- An **introduction** specific to the volume topic.
- For each viewpoint, a brief **introduction** that has notes about the author and source of the viewpoint, and that provides a summary of its main points.
- Full-color **charts**, **graphs**, **maps**, and other visual representations.

- Informational **sidebars** that explore the lives of key individuals, give background on historical events, or explain scientific or technical concepts.
- A **glossary** that defines key terms, as needed.
- A **chronology** of important dates preceding, during, and immediately following the event.
- A **bibliography** of additional books, periodicals, and Web sites for further research.
- A comprehensive **subject index** that offers access to people, places, and events cited in the text.

Perspectives on Modern World History is designed for a broad spectrum of readers who want to learn more about not only history but also current events, political science, government, international relations, and sociology—students doing research for class assignments or debates, teachers and faculty seeking to supplement course materials, and others wanting to improve their understanding of history. Each volume of Perspectives on Modern World History is designed to illuminate a complicated event, to spark debate, and to show the human perspective behind the world's most significant happenings of recent decades.

INTRODUCTION

Today, civil rights leader Martin Luther King, Jr., is a venerated figure admired by individuals from all parts of the political spectrum. However, during his lifetime, he was extremely controversial. Many people considered him a traitorous danger to the United States. One of King's most powerful and influential enemies was J. Edgar Hoover, the director of the Federal Bureau of Investigation (FBI).

In the 1950s and 1960s, the FBI set itself to monitor and disrupt the efforts of African Americans to gain equality and justice. "As the civil rights movement grew and expanded, the FBI pinpointed every group and emergent leader for intensive investigation and most for harassment and disruption," according to Morton Halperin, et al., in the 1976 monograph *The Lawless State: The Crimes of the U.S. Intelligence Agencies.*

As the most prominent civil rights figure, King was singled out as a target. The FBI's campaign against him was also fueled by Hoover's personal animosity toward King. Hoover had "determined as early as February 1962 that King was 'no good in any way,'" according to Peter Ling in his 2002 book *Martin Luther King, Jr.*

Hoover was convinced that the civil rights movement was permeated with, and instigated by, Communist agitators who were using the issue of black rights to undermine the United States. In particular, he believed that one of King's closest advisors, the Jewish businessman Stanley Levison, was a Communist plant. Levison had in fact been involved with the Communist Party, but appears to have abandoned that affiliation to work with King. In a letter to King as quoted in a July-August 2002 article in *Atlantic Monthly* by David J. Garrow,

Levison noted that the black "liberation struggle is the most positive and rewarding area of work anyone could experience."

By March 1963, according to Garrow, the FBI had "ironclad evidence that Levison had explicitly severed [all] remaining ties" with the Communist Party. However, the FBI "conveyed that crucial news to absolutely no one outside the Bureau, not even the Attorney General [Robert Kennedy]." Instead, Hoover and the FBI continued to maintain that Levison had ties to Communist organizations. They used this falsehood to convince Robert Kennedy in October 1963 to authorize an aggressive program of warrantless and illegal surveillance of King. The surveillance program started with phone taps and then escalated until agents were burglarizing King's hotel rooms to place wiretaps under his beds. King was also placed under direct surveillance by FBI agents.

The wiretaps clearly demonstrated that King was not a Communist. On tape in 1965, Garrow notes, he actually called communism "an alien philosophy contrary to us." The FBI never reported this to anyone outside the bureau either and instead continued to assert that King was a committed Communist and a danger to America.

Though the FBI had to lie about King's political sympathies, the wiretapping did disclose a different kind of impropriety: King was repeatedly unfaithful to his wife. The revelation of King's sexual exploits appears to have particularly angered Hoover, who became "obsessed with King's private life," according to Peter Ling. Ling also quotes Hoover as calling King "a 'tom cat' with obsessive sexual urges." The agent assigned to King, William Cornelius Sullivan, also personally insulted King, calling him a "beast" and an "animal" according to Michael Richardson in a January 15, 2009, article in the *Boston Progressive Examiner*.

It appears that the FBI not only tried to end King's career, but actually seems to have tried to push him to suicide. In an effort to destroy King, Sullivan made a compilation tape of King's sexual encounters obtained from the wiretaps. According to Richardson:

> The tape was played for members of Congress, supervisory personnel of the FBI, the President, Attorney General and dozens of reporters. Members of the clergy and even some of King's associates were given listening sessions. Sullivan had a copy of the sex tape made and sent to King from Florida along with an anonymous letter urging King to commit suicide to prevent public release of the tape.

The tape did not have the effect the FBI hoped: President Lyndon Johnson was amused rather than offended, reporters were not interested in the story, and King's wife Coretta continued to support him.

King died a few years later after being shot while on a Memphis hotel balcony on April 4, 1968. The FBI's animosity to King led some to suspect that the bureau or the government was directly involved in King's assassination. Speaking about the killing, Andrew Young, one of King's close associates, said that he "always thought that the FBI might be involved in some way," as quoted by Mark Gribben in an undated article on *Crime Library* on Trutv.com. William Pepper, who became the attorney for King's assassin, James Earl Ray, argues in his 2003 book, *An Act of State,* that a memo shows the FBI attempted to influence King's choice of hotel in Memphis. For Pepper, the implication is that the FBI helped to organize King's assassination.

In fact, Hoover was initially reluctant to take on the search for the civil rights leader's assassin, in part because of his hatred of King. Hoover acquiesced only after Attorney General William Ramsey Clark insisted that the FBI should be involved. The FBI's manhunt eventually became "the largest in American history, ultimately involving more than thirty-five hundred FBI agents and costing the government nearly two million dollars," according to Hampton Sides in his 2010 book, *Hellhound on His Trail: The Stalking of Martin Luther King, Jr. and the International Hunt for His Assassin*. Attorney General Clark even believed that Hoover's personal animosity towards King made the director more, not less, determined to catch the killer once the FBI had taken the case. Sides quotes Clark as saying:

> The FBI's reputation was at stake, and there was nothing more important to Hoover than the bureau's reputation. Hoover was afraid people were going to say *he* did it. So he was all out for finding the killer. And from the start you could feel it in the pace and the seriousness of the people in the bureau.

Ironically, one person who may have been pleased that the FBI had taken charge of the case was King's assassin, a man named James Earl Ray. Ray seems to have hoped that the assassination and an FBI investigation would make him famous, especially among other criminals. Before the assassination, Ray had an "oft-stated belief, even wish, that the FBI would place him on its ten most-wanted list," according to Gerald Posner in his 1998 book, *Killing the Dream: James Earl Ray and the Assassination of Martin Luther King Jr.* After he had killed King, according to Posner,

> Ray relished that newfound notoriety, even taking the risk, while on the run, of visiting a local bar in Toronto in order to watch the popular television program *The F.B.I.* on the night he was placed at the top of the Bureau's most-wanted list. After his arrest, he constantly asked the policemen assigned to guard him about the publicity over the case and how he was portrayed in the press.

While Ray may have been initially pleased with the FBI's involvement, he could not have been happy with the outcome of the investigation. The FBI captured him on June 8, 1968, while he was attempting to board a flight out of London's Heathrow Airport. Thus, the agency that had hounded King during his life ended up bringing his killer to justice.

World Map

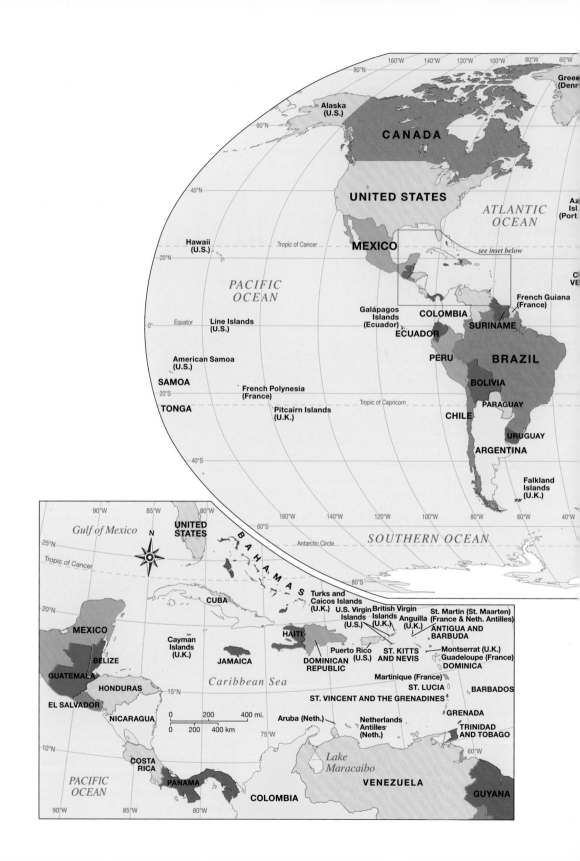

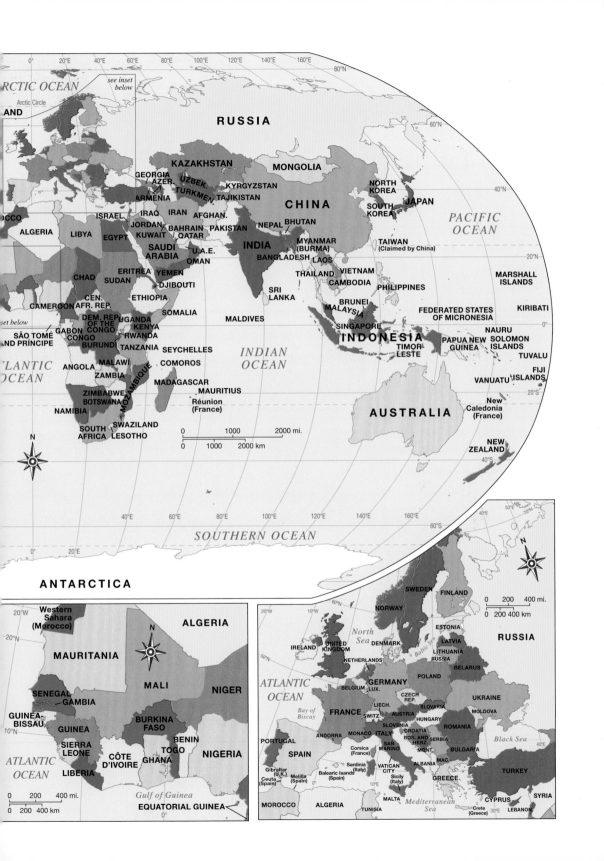

CHAPTER 1

Background on the Assassination of Martin Luther King, Jr.

The Life of Martin Luther King, Jr.

Contemporary Black Biography

The following entry from an encyclopedia detailing the lives of important African Americans provides a biography of Martin Luther King Jr., King is regarded as the most famous and influential leader of the struggle for black civil rights during the 1960s. He was involved in the Montgomery bus boycotts of 1955–56 that integrated that city's public transportation, in the successful 1963 Birmingham protests, and in the 1963 March on Washington, during which he delivered his famous "I Have a Dream" speech. He also opposed the Vietnam War, organized against poverty, and won the Nobel Peace Prize. He was assassinated in 1968.

Photo on previous page: Activist and clergyman Martin Luther King, Jr., reshaped the civil rights movement in the United States. (**Associated Press.**)

In the years since his assassination on April 4, 1968, as he stood on the balcony of the Lorraine Motel in Memphis, Tennessee, Martin Luther King, Jr., has evolved from a prominent civil rights leader into

SOURCE. "Martin Luther King Jr.," *Contemporary Black Biography*, Gale Research, 1992. Reproduced by permission.

the symbol for the civil rights movement in the United States. He is studied by schoolchildren of all backgrounds; his words are quoted by the powerless and the powerful, by anyone who has a dream to make her or his life better, to better the nation, or the world. Monuments have been dedicated in his honor and institutions such as the Center for Nonviolent Social Change in Atlanta which bears his name have been established to carry on his work. In 1986, the U.S. Congress made King unique among twentieth-century Americans by designating his birthday a federal holiday.

Vocation and Education

King was born into a family of Baptist ministers. . . . As the son of a pastor growing up among the black middle class, the young King was afforded some opportunities for education and experience not available to children in poorer urban and rural areas. Yet despite his social standing, he was still subjected to the lessons of segregation because of his color. Although his family tradition was intertwined with the church and expectations were high that "M. L." would follow in the footsteps of his father and grandfather, King first resisted the ministry as a vocation, finding it ill-suited to allow him to address the social problems he had experienced in the South. So, after completing high school early, he entered nearby Morehouse College in 1944 with thoughts of becoming a lawyer or doctor. Later, influenced by the teachings of George D. Kelsey, a religion professor, and Dr. Benjamin Mays, the college's president, King came to understand the social and intellectual tradition of the ministry. By graduation in 1948, he had decided to accept it as his vocation.

> It was . . . during [his time in seminary] that King first learned of the nonviolent activism of Mohandas Gandhi.

In 1948 King entered the Crozer Theological Seminary in Chester,

Pennsylvania. . . . It was also during this time that King first learned of the nonviolent activism of Mohandas Gandhi. . . . [For doctoral study] he chose to attend Boston University. . . .

The Montgomery Bus Boycott

[Upon emerging from Boston University, King] decided to accept the pastorship at Dexter Avenue Baptist Church in the Deep South of Montgomery, Alabama. He installed himself as full-time pastor in September of 1954. During his first year at Dexter, King finished his dissertation and worked to organize his new church, to activate the social and political awareness of his congregation, and to blend his academic learning with the emotional oratory of the Southern preacher. He had begun to settle into his role as preacher and new father when the events of December,

The timing and the manner of King's death help make him an indelible figure in history. (Simon Bruty/ Allsport/Getty Images.)

> King was arrested, slandered, received hate mail and phone threats, and his house was bombed; but from the outset he preached nonviolence.

1955, thrust upon him the mantle of local civil rights leader.

On December 1, 1955, Rosa Parks was arrested for refusing to abide by one of Montgomery's laws requiring segregated seating on city buses. In response to this incident, several groups within the city's black community, long dissatisfied with the treatment of blacks on public transportation, came together to take action. The NAACP [National Association for the Advancement of Colored People], the Women's Political Council, the Baptist Ministers Conference, the city's AME [African Methodist Episcopal] Zionist ministers, and the community at large united to organize a boycott of the buses. After a successful first day of boycotting, the groups formed the Montgomery Improvement Association [MIA] to oversee the community action and to work with the city and busline officials to bring about fairer treatment of blacks within the existing laws. King was elected the MIA's first president.

For 382 days, King and the black community maintained the boycott while white officials from the city and the busline resisted their modest demands: courtesy toward black riders, a first-come-first-serve approach to segregated seating, and black drivers for some routes. During this period, the MIA convinced black-owned taxis to reduce their fares to enable boycotters to afford a means of transportation. Then, when the city blocked that measure, the group organized carpools. King was arrested, slandered, received hate mail and phone threats, and his house was bombed; but from the outset he preached nonviolence to the black boycotters. After the Montgomery city officials refused to be moved to change by a number of related federal court decisions, the black community finally won more than it had asked for when the U.S. Supreme Court upheld a federal court decision that ruled against segregation in Montgomery. On December 21, 1956, the integration of Montgomery city buses became mandatory.

The SCLC

To continue the momentum gained from the victory in Montgomery and to spread the movement across the South, King and other black leaders gathered in early 1957 to form the Southern Christian Leadership Conference [SCLC]. As president of the SCLC, King spent the next few years consolidating the organization's position as a social force in the region and establishing himself as its leader. . . . With demands on his time growing, King decided to resign from the Dexter Avenue Baptist Church in Montgomery and to accept his father's offer to become co-pastor of the Ebenezer Baptist Church in Atlanta. This arrangement afforded the younger King the flexibility to devote more time to SCLC activities.

> [King's] efforts contributed to the eventual desegregation of stores, buses, and bus stations.

From 1960 to 1962 King and the SCLC renewed their direct action against segregation at the voting booth, at schools, at lunch counters, and at bus stations. King also threw his organization's support behind other groups fighting the same battles. . . . These efforts contributed to the eventual desegregation of stores, buses, and bus stations.

Yet, along with these successes, King and the civil rights movement also encountered failures. In December of 1961 the SCLC joined members of the black community of Albany, Georgia, in their effort to end segregation in that city. In the end, the white city government and the law enforcement officials refused to make any substantial concessions and avoided resorting to violence. The black organizations involved, on the other hand, were unable

The 1963 March on Washington

More than 200,000 Americans, most of them black but many of them white, demonstrated here today [August 28, 1963] for a full and speedy program of civil rights and equal job opportunities.

It was the greatest assembly for a redress of grievances that this capital has ever seen. . . .

On Capitol Hill, opinion was divided about the impact of the demonstration in stimulating Congressional action on civil rights legislation. . . .

The march leaders went from the shadows of the Lincoln Memorial to the White House to meet with the President for 75 minutes. Afterward, Mr. Kennedy issued a 400-word statement praising the marchers for the "deep fervor and the quiet dignity" that had characterized the demonstration.

SOURCE. *E.W. Kensworthy, "200,000 March for Civil Rights In Orderly Washington Rally; President Sees Gain for Negro,"* New York Times, *August 28, 1963.*

to cooperate among themselves and unable to keep Albany's blacks from turning to violence. With the failure in Albany, King's leadership and philosophy of nonviolence, as well as the SCLC's planning, came under criticism.

King was able to redeem himself in the spring of 1963 in Birmingham, Alabama, a city considered by many to be the most segregated in the country. King and the SCLC were invited by local black leaders to help them organize a protest to end segregation in downtown stores, to achieve equal opportunity in employment, and to establish a biracial commission to promote further desegregation. In order to attract attention to their demands and to put pressure on local businesses, the protesters employed the march. Birmingham police moved against the first march with clubs and attack dogs and the state court issued an injunction barring further protests. When King and close associate Ralph Abernathy defied the court order, they were arrested and placed in solitary confinement. During his incarceration, criticism by local white clergymen of the movement and King's actions prompted him to write his famous "Letter from a Birmingham Jail."

After being tried for contempt and found guilty, King was released on appeal. He rejoined the protesters. . . . The police brutality directed toward unarmed black men, women, and children outraged the nation and the [President John F.] Kennedy administration. The growing tide of negative publicity soon convinced Birmingham's white businessmen to seek an agreement with the protesters. . . .

The March on Washington

With the success of Birmingham still fresh in the minds of blacks and whites in the South and North, King was poised to assert himself as a national and international leader. On August 28, 1963, approximately 250,000 blacks and whites marched on Washington, D.C., to raise the nation's consciousness of civil rights and to encourage the passage of the Civil Rights Bill before Congress at that time. The march was a cooperative effort of several civil rights organizations . . . and the movement's largest demonstration. King was the last speaker scheduled to address the crowd gathered in the shadow of the Lincoln Memorial. He began a speech that referred to the lack of progress in securing black rights in the hundred years since Lincoln's Emancipation Proclamation; by the time he finished, he had deviated from his prepared speech to offer a speech drawn from past sermons and from the inspiration of the moment, his famous "I Have a Dream" address.

King's stature as a leader of national and international prominence was confirmed in 1964. In January of that year he became the first black American to be named *Time* magazine's "Man of the Year." And, in December of that year he was awarded the Nobel Peace Prize, the youngest person ever to win the award. . . . Earlier in 1964 [King] had attended the signing of the Civil Rights Act of 1964, the law that had put the federal government firmly behind ending segregation and discrimination in public institutions. But blacks still faced barriers to voting throughout the South, and they faced more subtle economic barriers in other regions.

In 1965 and 1966 King and the SCLC decided to take on these barriers. Civil rights groups stepped up their voter registration drives in the South and King took his strategy of nonviolent confrontation to Selma, Alabama. Marches in Selma and from Selma to the state capital of Montgomery brought publicity to the movement's voting rights demands and gave momentum to congressional efforts to enact legislation to remedy the situation. In August, the Voting Rights Act of 1965 was passed into law. It gave federal authorities the power to end literacy tests and poll taxes and to monitor all elections.

In 1966 King and the SCLC launched a campaign in Chicago, both to expand their influence into the North and to raise awareness of the issues of urban discrimination and poverty as manifested in housing, schooling, and unemployment. The SCLC influenced some changes and put some long-term operations in place such as Operation Breadbasket. However, the campaign was unable to score the kind of success that it had in Montgomery, Birmingham, and Selma. Discrimination was more subtle in this northern metropolis than in the segregated South; city officials, including Mayor Richard Daley, were less extreme and more politically astute than their southern counterparts in their response to confrontation; further-more, Chicago's black population was more divided, with some elements very much prone to violence.

Vietnam and Poverty

In the last year of his life, King actively expanded the scope of his efforts to include not only civil rights issues but also human rights issues important to people the world over. As the war in Vietnam escalated in the second half of the 1960s, King had grown dissatisfied with the situation. In 1967 he began to speak out consistently against the war. . . .

Late in 1967 King directed his organization to begin laying the groundwork for what would be known as the Poor People's Campaign. He wanted to recruit the poor from urban and rural areas—men and women of all races and backgrounds—and lead them in a campaign for economic rights. The recruited poor, trained in nonviolent direct action, would descend on Washington, D.C., and begin a three-month campaign of marches, rallies, sit-ins, and boycotts to pressure the [President Lyndon] Johnson administration and leading businessmen to put a more human face on American capitalism.

In March of 1968, while touring the U.S. to raise support for this new march on Washington, King accepted an invitation to speak on behalf of sanitation workers in Memphis, Tennessee, who were striking in an attempt to improve their poor working conditions. After a march organized by local leaders was postponed because of a heavy snowstorm, King joined the rescheduled event on March 28. Shortly after the march began, young gang members initiated violence, igniting a riot that ended with one dead, numerous injuries, and widespread property damage. King vowed to return to personally direct another demonstration in order to reestablish nonviolence in this local dispute.

Again in Memphis to plan this march, King was assassinated on April 4, 1968, as he stood on the balcony of the Lorraine Motel.

In His Last Year, Martin Luther King Was a Controversial Figure

Kate Ellis and Stephen Smith

Kate Ellis is a producer and Stephen Smith is an executive editor and host with American RadioWorks. In the following viewpoint, a transcript of an hour-long radio program, they describe the difficulties faced by Martin Luther King, Jr., in his last year. During that time, King was involved in a number of controversial initiatives. First, he began to vocally oppose the Vietnam War, drawing the ire of the FBI and President Lyndon Johnson. King also began to work with the Poor People's Campaign to organize a march on Washington, D.C., for economic justice. Finally, he became involved in a volatile and sometimes violent sanitation workers' strike in Memphis, Tennessee.

SOURCE. Kate Ellis and Stephen Smith, "King's Last March," American Public Media's "American RadioWorks," ®, © 2008 American Public Media. Used with permission. All rights reserved. Reprinted by arrangement with The Heirs to the Estate of Martin Luther King Jr., c/o Writers House as agent for the proprietor New York, NY. Copyright © 1963 Dr. Martin Luther King Jr; copyright renewed 1991 by Coretta Scott King.

Four decades after Martin Luther King Jr. was assassinated [in 1968], he remains one of the most vivid symbols of hope for racial unity in America. But that's not the way he was viewed the last year of his life. . . .

I'm Stephen Smith. . . .

Standing Against the War

This is Riverside Church in New York City. It's a classic, Gothic cathedral, with light spilling down from stained glass windows and pointed arches reaching up into a vaulted ceiling. It's a formal, elegant place. It was here at Riverside Church four decades ago that the Reverend Martin Luther King Jr. gave one of the most radical and controversial speeches of his life. He called for an end to the Vietnam War.

> *King*: Now it should be incandescently clear that no one who has any concern for the integrity and life of America today can ignore the present war. If America's soul becomes totally poisoned, part of the autopsy must read: Vietnam.

These words placed King well to the left of the American mainstream at the time. The anti-war movement was just gathering steam. Most Americans still supported fighting on to victory. King spoke here at Riverside Church on April 4th, 1967. Exactly one year later, he was assassinated. . . .

Now if the somber-sounding Martin Luther King who spoke at Riverside Church isn't the towering orator you're used to hearing, stay with me. In the last year of his life, King was, in many ways, not the figure that both his followers and his opponents had come to know. He could still thunder from the pulpit, for sure, but his message grew more challeng-

> " In the last year of [King's] life . . . his message grew more challenging, and more pessimistic. "

ing, and more pessimistic. Back in 1963, King stirred the nation with his "I Have a Dream" speech from the steps of the Lincoln Memorial. In 1967, he lamented what had become of that dream.

> *King*: I talked in Washington in 1963 about my dream. And we stood there on those high moments with high hopes. And over and over again I've seen this dream turn into a nightmare! I've seen promising, young, black boys, who are already facing discrimination at home, going away and dying in disproportionate numbers in Vietnam. We are 11 percent of the population here, and we are 22 and 4/10 percent of the dying force in Vietnam!

Over the coming hour we'll trace the final year of King's life. It was a time when a hostile U.S. government spied on King, and neglected to warn him about death threats being made against him; a time when King followed his moral compass to an increasingly isolated and lonely place; and a time when his deep convictions about nonviolence and the need to help poor people led him to say things many Americans found threatening. But King said being morally wise sometimes meant being politically un-wise.

> *King*: On some positions, cowardice asks the question "Is it safe?" Expediency asks the question "Is it politic?" Vanity asks the question "Is it popular?" But conscience asks the question "Is it right?" And there comes a time when a man must take the position that is neither safe, nor politic, nor popular, but he must take it because it is right. And that's where I stand today!

Hard Questions

There were a lot of hard questions facing America in 1967. The country was beginning to feel the rumblings of a cultural earthquake. Anti-war movements, social justice movements, counter-culture movements—they were all converging to assault the status-quo. . . .

In the spring of 1967, more than 400,000 U.S. troops were stationed in Vietnam. At least a hundred American soldiers were dying each week in combat. . . .

> King's speeches against the Vietnam War drew swift public reaction, much of it damning.

President Lyndon Johnson had been escalating U.S. involvement in Vietnam since 1965. Martin Luther King had always opposed the war. But he'd been careful not to criticize it too sharply because Johnson had been a crucial ally on civil rights and on efforts to fight poverty. But as Johnson poured more troops into Vietnam, King felt compelled to speak out. . . .

Martin Luther King's speeches against the Vietnam War drew swift public reaction, much of it damning. Newspaper editorials chastised King for stepping outside his field of expertise: Civil Rights.

Michael Honey: You have to remember, in 1967, public opinion had not yet turned against the Vietnam War.

Historian Michael Honey wrote a book about King's last year of life, called *Going Down Jericho Road*.

Honey: The *New York Times*, for instance, virtually called him a traitor, saying he had undercut his usefulness to his people and his country by making that speech. . . . So he was roundly condemned, and within the black community too, by many black leaders. . . .

Some of King's staffers at the SCLC [Southern Christian Leadership Conference] doubted his decision to speak against the government and the war. Dorothy Cotton directed educational programs for the organization. She says King was pained by the criticism he got.

Dorothy Cotton: But I saw this pushing Martin into a

kind of reflective mode, to really think about his own commitment, not in any way doubting it, but if he doubted it, he came out of it saying, and this is a direct quote, "If I am the last, lone voice speaking for nonviolence, that I will do."

King: Now there are those who say, "You're a Civil Rights leader. What are you doing speaking out? You should stay in your field." Well I wish you would go back and tell them for me that before I became a Civil Rights leader, I was a preacher of the Gospel. And when my father and others put their hands on my head and ordained me to the Christian ministry, it was a commission and something said to me that the fire of truth is shut up in my bones, and when it burns me, I must tell it!

The President and the FBI

When King spoke that "fire of truth" about Vietnam, it drew criticism, but also admiration, especially from people in the blossoming peace movement. In May 1967, King spoke to a crowd of 7,000 people on the campus of the University of California, Berkeley.

Student: Dr. King, will you be our candidate in 1968?

King: Well I must say, it's very kind of you to express such concern and make such a request. Now I do not feel that I'm presidential timber. I am committed to trying to do this job of civil rights and this job of building, wherever we can, more opposition to the war in Vietnam, and this would certainly take all of my time. And I would rather think of myself as one trying desperately to be the conscience of all of the political parties rather than being a political candidate.

Whether or not King could actually win the 1968 election, such speculation was deeply threatening to the incumbent Democrat, President Lyndon Johnson [LBJ].

LBJ was furious that King had broken ranks with him over the war. King's long-time nemesis, FBI Director J. Edgar Hoover, encouraged the president's anger. Hoover's FBI began spying on King and the SCLC back in 1962. Journalist Nick Kotz wrote a book about LBJ and King called *Judgment Days*. He says the bureau suspected that King and his organization were influenced by communists.

> *Nick Kotz*: J. Edgar Hoover was sending Johnson virtually a message a day telling him that King was a communist; that King's personal life was a mess; he had all kinds of extramarital affairs. And up until the Riverside speech, in April of '67, Johnson never did anything to strike out at King. With that speech, Johnson began to lash out at King, but privately. He never, ever did it publicly. And he was listening to Hoover's poison with a more attentive ear. . . .

> "[J. Edgar] Hoover was a racist, and he viewed King's growing activism . . . as a threat to the government."

King's massive FBI file contains no credible evidence that he was influenced by communists. But Hoover was a racist, and he viewed King's growing activism on both Vietnam and poverty as a threat to the government. So the FBI continued tapping King's phones, bugging his house, and in many other ways, trailing and reporting on King. [King's supporter and friend] Andrew Young said King and his colleagues in the movement knew they were being followed.

> *Andrew Young*: Whenever we checked into a hotel, we always saw the little cars with the guys. And they were always driving two-, three-year-old Plymouths. It was not hard to find them. Quite often, we found bugs in the hotel rooms. And we never moved them.

Young says they even found microphones hidden in church pulpits where King was scheduled to speak.

Young: I can remember Ralph Abernathy pulling one out and [saying], "Little doohickey, I don't know whether you [are] playing in Lyndon Johnson's office, or J. Edgar Hoover's office, but I want the whole world to know that we're going to get the right to vote and we're going to be free." And then he put it on top of the pulpit, rather than under the bottom, because he said, "I want you to get this plain."

For years, Hoover's FBI had been running a smear campaign against King. The bureau circulated reports about communists in King's camp and rumors about King's sex life. By 1967, about all King could do was try to ignore the threatening cloud of Hoover's skullduggery. King had much more difficult things on his mind.

Rioting and Poverty

In July of '67, violence tore at black neighborhoods in several American cities including Newark, New Jersey. . . .

When the Newark rioting ended, 23 people were dead. More than a thousand were in jail. An even bigger riot engulfed Detroit weeks later. Black people in America's inner cities were fed up with poverty and police repression. Young, militant activists seemed to dismiss Martin Luther King's message of nonviolence. . . .

> King had come to a depressing realization: the victories of a few years earlier . . . had not done much to make economic conditions better for most African Americans.

Over the summer of '67, King's mood darkened as his pessimism about the nation's racial and economic problems grew deeper. . . .

King had come to a depressing realization: the victories of a few years earlier, passage of the Civil Rights and Voting Rights Acts, had not done much to make economic conditions better for most African Americans. In private conversations, King despaired that he lacked the ideas and the energy to lift America from its darkness. . . .

Instead of escaping, King took on a daunting challenge. In the last year of his life, he called for a new phase to the civil rights movement—a campaign to finally wipe out poverty. . . .

In a series of speeches, King said the fight against poverty would be a much harder battle than the movement for racial justice. The struggle for economic justice would require far greater sacrifice from white America.

> *King*: It didn't cost the nation one penny to integrate lunch counters. It didn't cost the nation one penny to guarantee the right to vote. And the things that we are calling for now would mean that the nation will have to spend billions of dollars in order to solve these problems. In other words, we are in a period where there cannot be a solution to the problem without a radical redistribution of economic and political power.

It seemed to some people that King was becoming more radical. Certainly the FBI thought so. It cranked up its smear campaign against King by circulating bogus stories to news organizations about the civil rights leader. But historian Clayborne Carson says King wasn't more radical—he was returning to his ideological roots. Carson directs the King Papers Project at Stanford University. He says King saw himself first and foremost as a minister of the "social gospel," which meant:

> *Clayborne Carson*: One has a duty to do justice to the poor, to the less fortunate. That's the consistent message going from the Old Testament prophets through Jesus and into the modern world, and what Christians hope to bring to that world. So nothing could've been more central to his mission as a minister than to launch the Poor People's Campaign.

A Time to Break Silence

One of the greatest speeches by Martin Luther King, Jr., "A Time to Break Silence," was delivered at Riverside Church, New York City, on April 4, 1967. It is a statement against war. . . . Yet . . . it protests the command and deployment by [President] Lyndon Johnson of almost unlimited violence against the people and the land of Vietnam for the declared purpose of protecting them from the menace of world communism. . . .

This speech was King's public announcement of his opposition to the war. Moral protest, which said "The war is wrong," was still, as it would remain, very much a minority position. Even the tactical objection that said, "The war cannot be won," was still a marginal view, though now steadily gaining adherents. King knew that his uncompromising dissent would draw bitter attacks. Members of the black community would charge that by his new commitment he was diluting the single-minded pursuit of civil rights for which he was known to stand. "Some of us," he confesses, "who have already begun to break the silence of the night have found that the calling to speak is often a vocation of agony, but we must speak."

SOURCE. *David Bromwich, "Martin Luther King's Speech Against the Vietnam War," Antiwar.com, May 16, 2008. www.antiwar.com.*

The Poor People's Campaign was King's audacious plan to lead waves of poor people to Washington to set up a shanty town on the National Mall to show people in power the faces of the poor.

King: This will be no mere one-day march in Washington but a trek to the nation's capital by suffering and outraged citizens who will go to stay until some definite and positive action is taken to provide jobs and income for the poor. . . .

Memphis

In spring 1968, Martin Luther King Jr. got diverted from his work on the Poor People's Campaign by a garbage strike in Tennessee. . . .

Black sanitation workers were protesting against miserable working conditions. For years they carried garbage from backyard trash cans in round, steel tubs on their heads. Many tubs leaked. The men drank water from a cooler on the truck because they weren't allowed to stop for refreshment. Sometimes they found maggots in their drinking cups. . . .

Historian Michael Honey says the garbage workers put up with the wretched conditions until 1968, when two of their own suffered a gruesome accident. In Memphis, black trash haulers were not allowed to ride in the truck's cab with white workers. So when it rained, they often climbed in the back where the garbage cans got emptied. In back was also where the trash got crushed by a powerful blade.

Honey: On February 1, Echol Cole and Robert Walker, 36 and 30 years old, were riding in the back and the mechanism went off and went into action. The driver stopped the truck, but by the time he got out of the truck, the packing mechanism had grabbed them and mashed them just like garbage and they were killed instantly.

Black workers decided to strike. But city officials refused to bargain with the workers. And when peaceful demonstrators marched to city hall, police attacked them with tear gas and billy clubs. A month into the strike, [local organizer] James Lawson asked King to come to Memphis to boost morale. King arrived on March 18,

1968, and spoke to a massive crowd at the Mason Temple, a Pentecostal church. . . .

At first, King didn't plan to do more in Memphis than give this speech. In fact, his staff at the SCLC didn't want him to go at all. Andrew Young ran the organization's daily operations. Young feared that Memphis would be a troublesome detour on the road to the SCLC's poor people's march in Washington. . . .

> King's visit to Memphis lifted morale among the strikers and their supporters.

King's visit to Memphis lifted morale among the strikers and their supporters. But it was also a tonic for King. At the time, King was struggling to recruit people for the Washington march. And his popularity seemed to be ebbing. But the Mason Temple was one of the largest gathering places for black people in the South, and as many as 14,000 packed the place to hear King speak. . . .

Violence Erupts

King promised the strikers in Memphis he would come back soon and help reach that high-water mark. Instead, when he returned, King would endure one of the lowest days of his civil rights career.

> *Reporter 1*: Dr. Martin Luther King's massive downtown march on Memphis is now under way. Several thousand Negroes are marching towards city hall at this time.

March 28, 1968. King is back in Memphis. This time, he's accompanied by just two of his staffers from the SCLC. . . .

Though King steps up to lead the protest march, he's counting on local organizers to keep the demonstration orderly. Michael Honey says King is obviously uneasy as he's pushed along by the crowd.

> *Honey*: You can see in the photography of the march that

Dr. King is visibly exhausted. His head is falling from side to side; he looks dazed. He looks apprehensive. He's not feeling like he's really in control of the situation, and he really isn't. . . .

The violence begins in the crowd behind King as he and the march leaders turn a corner onto Memphis' main street. Local organizer, James Lawson, was with King. . . .

Lawson says he saw a dozen or so young people breaking store front windows. But the riot police weren't interested in them.

Lawson: And I point up the street, and I say, "They're going to break the march up."

Reporter 1: Police have formed a cordon across Main Street at this time in an attempt to at least calm the demonstration, which has gotten completely out of hand. The Negro youths are shouting at this time, "Go! Go! Go!"

Honey: James Lawson's response was, "Martin, they're coming for you, the police. Secondly, you can't be in the position of leading a march that leads to violence." So Lawson got him out of the march. And King protested. Because he knew that people would say he ran, and so forth, which the news media did say.

Reporter 2: Was that Martin Luther King? He has deserted the march? He has left the march? And Martin Luther King has left the march. We're waiting on the rest of our crew here.

The violence continued for hours as peaceful marchers got caught up in the same police counterattack as looters. One teenager was shot to death. Dozens of protestors were injured, and nearly 300 black people arrested. Stores in the black section of town got looted and burned.

Martin Luther King was despondent. He crawled into bed at his Memphis hotel with his clothes on, trying to sort out what had gone wrong and what to do next. He spent the evening with SCLC staff who had hurried to Memphis. . . .

When he got home to Atlanta, King told his staff at the SCLC there was no choice: he would have to return to Memphis. King said he had to prove he could lead a nonviolent demonstration in Memphis before moving on to Washington. Again, some on the staff objected. But King was adamant. And six days later he was back in Memphis, this time with a full team of SCLC organizers. It was April 3, 1968.

Martin Luther King Speaks to a Crowd the Day Before His Assassination

Martin Luther King, Jr.

> Martin Luther King, Jr., delivered his last speech on April 3, 1968, in Memphis, Tennessee, the day before his assassination. In the speech he talks about nonviolent and economic tactics to resolve the Memphis sanitation workers' strike. He also states that he feels lucky to have participated in the struggle for justice and freedom. He adds that even if he does not live a long life, he is satisfied in knowing that he has followed the will of God and that the struggle will be successful.

SOURCE. Martin Luther King Jr., "I've Been to the Mountaintop," *American Rhetoric*, April 3, 1968. Reproduced by permission.

Something is happening in Memphis; something is happening in our world. And you know, if I were standing at the beginning of time, with the possibility of taking a kind of general and panoramic view of the whole of human history up to now, and the Almighty said to me, "Martin Luther King, which age would you like to live in?" . . .

> 'If you allow me to live just a few years in the second half of the 20th century, I will be happy.'

Strangely enough, I would turn to the Almighty, and say, "If you allow me to live just a few years in the second half of the 20th century, I will be happy."

Now that's a strange statement to make, because the world is all messed up. The nation is sick. Trouble is in the land; confusion all around. That's a strange statement. But I know, somehow, that only when it is dark enough can you see the stars. And I see God working in this period of the twentieth century in a way that men, in some strange way, are responding.

Something is happening in our world. The masses of people are rising up. And wherever they are assembled today, whether they are in Johannesburg, South Africa; Nairobi, Kenya; Accra, Ghana; New York City; Atlanta, Georgia; Jackson, Mississippi; or Memphis, Tennessee—the cry is always the same: "We want to be free."

And another reason that I'm happy to live in this period is that we have been forced to a point where we are going to have to grapple with the problems that men have been trying to grapple with through history, but the demands didn't force them to do it. Survival demands that we grapple with them. Men, for years now, have been talking about war and peace. But now, no longer can they just talk about it. It is no longer a choice between violence and nonviolence in this world; it's nonviolence or nonexistence. That is where we are today.

Forty years after King's death, marchers in Memphis recalled the strike that brought him to the city in 1968. (Getty Images.)

And also in the human rights revolution, if something isn't done, and done in a hurry, to bring the colored peoples of the world out of their long years of poverty, their long years of hurt and neglect, the whole world is doomed. Now, I'm just happy that God has allowed me to live in this period to see what is unfolding. And I'm happy that He's allowed me to be in Memphis.

I can remember—I can remember when Negroes were just going around as Ralph [Abernathy, leader of the Southern Christian Leadership Council, or SCLC] has said, so often, scratching where they didn't itch, and laughing when they were not tickled. But that day is all over. We mean business now, and we are determined to gain our rightful place in God's world.

And that's all this whole thing is about. We aren't engaged in any negative protest and in any negative arguments with anybody. We are saying that we are determined to be men. We are determined to be people. We are saying—We are saying that we are God's children. And that we don't have to live like we are forced to live.

> We are saying that we are God's children. And that we don't have to live like we are forced to live.

Now, what does all of this mean in this great period of history? It means that we've got to stay together. We've got to stay together and maintain unity. You know, whenever Pharaoh wanted to prolong the period of slavery in Egypt, he had a favorite, favorite formula for doing it. What was that? He kept the slaves fighting among themselves. But whenever the slaves get together, something happens in Pharaoh's court, and he cannot hold the slaves in slavery. When the slaves get together, that's the beginning of getting out of slavery. Now let us maintain unity.

Secondly, let us keep the issues where they are. The issue is injustice. The issue is the refusal of Memphis to be fair and honest in its dealings with its public servants, who happen to be sanitation workers. Now, we've got to keep attention on that. That's always the problem with a little violence. You know what happened the other day, and the press dealt only with the window-breaking. I read the articles. They very seldom got around to mentioning the fact that one thousand, three hundred sanitation workers are on strike, and that Memphis is not being fair to them. . . .

Now we're going to march again, and we've got to march again, in order to put the issue where it is supposed to be—and force everybody to see that there are thirteen hundred of God's children here suffering, sometimes going hungry, going through dark and dreary nights wondering how this thing is going to come out. That's the issue. And we've got to say to the nation: We know how it's coming out. For when people get caught up with that which is right and they are willing to sacrifice for it, there is no stopping point short of victory.

> Individually, we are poor when you compare us with white society. . . . Collectively we are richer than [almost] all the nations in the world.

We aren't going to let any mace stop us. We are masters in our nonviolent movement in disarming police forces; they don't know what to do. I've seen them so often. I remember in Birmingham, Alabama, when we were in that majestic struggle there, we would move out of the 16th Street Baptist Church day after day; by the hundreds we would move out. And Bull Connor [the police chief] would tell them to send the dogs forth, and they did come; but we just went before the dogs singing, "Ain't gonna let nobody turn me around." . . .

Now the other thing we'll have to do is this: Always anchor our external direct action with the power of economic withdrawal. Now, we are poor people. Individually, we are poor when you compare us with white society in America. We are poor. Never stop and forget that collectively—that means all of us together—collectively we are richer than all the nations in the world, with the exception of nine. Did you ever think about that? After you leave the United States, Soviet Russia, Great Britain, West Germany, France, and I could name the others, the American Negro collectively is richer than most nations of the world. We have an annual income of more than thirty billion dollars a year, which is more than all of the exports of the United States, and more than the national budget of Canada. Did you know that? That's power right there, if we know how to pool it.

We don't have to argue with anybody. We don't have to curse and go around acting bad with our words. We don't need any bricks and bottles. We don't need any Molotov cocktails. We just need to go around to these stores, and to these massive industries in our country, and say, "God sent us by here, to say to you that you're not treating his children right. And we've come by here to ask you to make the first item on your agenda fair treatment, where God's children are concerned. Now, if you are not prepared to do that, we do have an agenda that we must follow. And our agenda calls for withdrawing economic support from you."

And so, as a result of this, we are asking you tonight, to go out and tell your neighbors not to buy Coca-Cola in Memphis. Go by and tell them not to buy Sealtest milk. Tell them not to buy—what is the other bread?—Wonder Bread. And what is the other bread company, Jesse? Tell them not to buy Hart's bread. As [civil rights leader] Jesse Jackson has said, up to now, only the garbage men have been feeling pain; now we must kind of redistribute the pain. We are choosing these companies because they haven't been fair in their hiring policies; and we are choosing them because they can begin the process of saying they are going to support the needs and the rights of these men who are on strike. And then they can move on town—downtown and tell Mayor [Henry] Loeb to do what is right.

But not only that, we've got to strengthen black institutions. I call upon you to take your money out of the banks downtown and deposit your money in Tri-State Bank. We want a "bank-in" movement in Memphis. Go by the savings and loan association. I'm not asking you something that we don't do ourselves at SCLC. Judge [Benjamin] Hooks and others will tell you that we have an account here in the savings and loan association from the Southern Christian Leadership Conference. We are telling you to follow what we are doing. Put your money there. You have six or seven black insurance companies here in the city of Memphis. Take out your insurance there. We want to have an "insurance-in."

Now these are some practical things that we can do. We begin the process of building a greater economic base. And at the same time, we are putting pressure where it really hurts. I ask you to follow through here.

> "Let us develop a kind of dangerous unselfishness."

Now, let me say as I move to my conclusion that we've got to give ourselves to this struggle until the end. Nothing would be more tragic than to stop at this point in Memphis. We've got to see it through. And when we have our march, you need to be there. If it means leaving work, if it means leaving school—be there. Be concerned about your brother. You may not be on strike. But either we go up together, or we go down together.

Let us develop a kind of dangerous unselfishness. One day a man came to Jesus, and he wanted to raise some questions about some vital matters of life. At points he wanted to trick Jesus, and show him that he knew a little more than Jesus knew and throw him off base.[1] . . .

Now that question could have easily ended up in a philosophical and theological debate. But Jesus immediately pulled that question from mid-air, and placed it on a dangerous curve between Jerusalem and Jericho.[2] And he talked about a certain man, who fell among thieves. You remember that a Levite [a member of the tribe of Levi] and a priest passed by on the other side. They didn't stop to help him. And finally a man of another race came by. He got down from his beast, decided not to be compassionate by proxy. But he got down with him, administered first aid, and helped the man in need. Jesus ended up saying, this was the good man, this was the great man, because he had the capacity to project the "I" into the "thou," and to be concerned about his brother.

Now you know, we use our imagination a great deal to try to determine why the priest and the Levite didn't stop. At times we say they were busy going to a church meeting, an ecclesiastical gathering, and they had to get on down to Jerusalem so they wouldn't be late for their meeting. At other times we would speculate that there was a religious law that "One who was engaged in religious ceremonials was not to touch a human body twenty-four hours before the ceremony." And every now and then we begin to wonder whether maybe they were not going down to Jerusalem—or down to Jericho, rather to organize a "Jericho Road Improvement Association." That's a possibility. Maybe they felt that it was better to deal with the problem from the causal root, rather than to get bogged down with an individual effect.

But I'm going to tell you what my imagination tells me. It's possible that those men were afraid. You see, the Jericho road is a dangerous road. I remember when Mrs. [Coretta Scott] King and I were first in Jerusalem. We rented a car and drove from Jerusalem down to Jericho. And as soon as we got on that road, I said to my wife, "I can see why Jesus used this as the setting for his parable." It's a winding, meandering road. It's really conducive for ambushing. You start out in Jerusalem, which is about 1200 miles—or rather 1200 feet above sea level. And by the time you get down to Jericho, fifteen or twenty minutes later, you're about 2200 feet below sea level. That's a dangerous road. In the days of Jesus it came to be known as the "Bloody Pass." And you know, it's possible that the priest and the Levite looked over that man on the ground and wondered if the robbers were still around. Or it's possible that they felt that the man on the ground was merely faking. And he was acting like he had been robbed and hurt, in order to seize them over there, lure them there for quick and easy seizure. And so the first question that the priest asked—the first question that the Levite asked was, "If I stop to help this man, what will happen to me?" But then the Good Samaritan came by. And he reversed the question: "If I do not stop to help this man, what will happen to him?"

That's the question before you tonight. Not, "If I stop to help the sanitation workers, what will happen to my job?" Not, "If I stop to help the sanitation workers what will happen to all of the hours that I usually spend in my office every day and every week as a pastor?" The question is not, "If I stop to help this man in need, what will happen to me?" The question is, "If I do not stop to help the sanitation workers, what will happen to them?" That's the question.

Let us rise up tonight with a greater readiness. Let us stand with a greater determination. And let us move on in these powerful days, these days of challenge to make America what it ought to be. We have an opportunity to make America a better nation. And I want to thank God, once more, for allowing me to be here with you.

You know, several years ago, I was in New York City autographing the first book that I had written. And while sitting there autographing books, a demented black woman came up. The only question I heard from her was, "Are you Martin Luther King?" And I was looking down writing, and I said, "Yes." And the next minute I felt something beating on my chest. Before I knew it I had been stabbed by this demented woman. I was rushed to Harlem Hospital. It was a dark Saturday afternoon. And that blade had gone through, and the x-rays revealed that the tip of the blade was on the edge of my aorta, the main artery. And once that's punctured, you're drowned in your own blood—that's the end of you.

It came out in the *New York Times* the next morning, that if I had merely sneezed, I would have died. Well, about four days later, they allowed me, after the operation, after my chest had been opened, and the blade had been taken out, to move around in the wheel chair in the hospital. They allowed me to read some of the mail that came in, and from all over the states and the world, kind letters came in. I read a few, but one of them I will never forget. I had received one from the President and the Vice-President. I've forgotten what those telegrams said. I'd received a visit and a letter from the Governor of New York, but I've forgotten what that letter said. But there was another letter that came from a little girl, a young girl who was a student at the White Plains High School. And I looked at that letter, and I'll never forget it. It said simply,

> Dear Dr. King,

> I am a ninth-grade student at the White Plains High School.

And she said,

> While it should not matter, I would like to mention that I'm a white girl. I read in the paper of your misfortune, and of your suffering. And I read that if you had sneezed, you would have died. And I'm simply writing you to say that I'm so happy that you didn't sneeze.

And I want to say tonight—I want to say tonight that I too am happy that I didn't sneeze. Because if I had sneezed, I wouldn't have been around here in 1960, when students all over the South started sitting in at lunch counters. And I knew that as they were sitting in, they were really standing up for the best in the American dream, and taking the whole nation back to those great wells of democracy which were dug deep by the Founding Fathers in the Declaration of Independence and the Constitution.

If I had sneezed, I wouldn't have been around here in 1961, when we decided to take a ride for freedom and ended segregation in inter-state travel.

If I had sneezed, I wouldn't have been around here in 1962, when Negroes in Albany, Georgia, decided to straighten their backs up. And whenever men and women straighten their backs up, they are going somewhere, because a man can't ride your back unless it is bent.

If I had sneezed—If I had sneezed I wouldn't have been here in 1963, when the black people of Birmingham, Alabama, aroused the conscience of this nation, and brought into being the Civil Rights Bill.

If I had sneezed, I wouldn't have had a chance later that year, in August, to try to tell America about a dream that I had had.

If I had sneezed, I wouldn't have been down in Selma, Alabama, to see the great Movement there.

If I had sneezed, I wouldn't have been in Memphis to see a community rally around those brothers and sisters who are suffering.

I'm so happy that I didn't sneeze.

And they were telling me—. Now, it doesn't matter, now. It really doesn't matter what happens now. I left Atlanta this morning, and as we got started on the plane, there were six of us. The pilot said over the public address system, "We are sorry for the delay, but we have Dr. Martin Luther King on the plane. And to be sure that all of the bags were checked, and to be sure that nothing would be wrong with the plane, we had to check out everything carefully. And we've had the plane protected and guarded all night."

> Like anybody, I would like to live a long life. . . . But I'm not concerned about that now. I just want to do God's will.

And then I got into Memphis. And some began to say the threats, or talk about the threats that were out. What would happen to me from some of our sick white brothers?

Well, I don't know what will happen now. We've got some difficult days ahead. But it really doesn't matter with me now, because I've been to the mountaintop.

And I don't mind.

Like anybody, I would like to live a long life. Longevity has its place. But I'm not concerned about that now. I just want to do God's will. And He's allowed me to go up to the mountain. And I've looked over. And I've seen the Promised Land. I may not get there with you. But I want you to know tonight, that we, as a people, will get to the promised land!

And so I'm happy, tonight.

I'm not worried about anything.

I'm not fearing any man!

Mine eyes have seen the glory of the coming of the Lord!!

Notes

1. King is referring to Luke 10:25–37, the parable of the Good Samaritan. A man noted that the law said to love thy neighbor as thyself then asked Jesus, "And who is my neighbor?"
2. In the parable of the Good Samaritan, a traveler is going from Jerusalem to Jericho when he is attacked by thieves.

Details Emerge of the Assassin's Plot

William Sorrels

William Wright Sorrels (1924–2008) was a journalist and author who worked for numerous publications, including the Memphis (TN) *Commercial Appeal* and *Life*. Beginning in 1984, he taught journalism at the Mississippi University for Women. In the following newspaper article published in Memphis two days after the assassination of Martin Luther King, Jr., Sorrels reports that a man calling himself "John Willard" rented an apartment in Memphis with a view of King's room. "Willard"—later identified as James Earl Ray—appears to have shot King and then escaped, though Sorrels notes that the authorities had many leads and seemed likely to apprehend the alleged assassin.

D r. Martin Luther King Jr.'s assassin said his name was John Willard.

He spoke with a Southern drawl.

SOURCE. William Sorrels, "Room 5 Was 'Fine' For Assassin's Plan," *Commercial Appeal*, April 6, 1968. Reproduced by permission.

He paid for his . . . room with a crisp $20 bill, fishing it out of his right front pocket and holding it in both hands before handing it to the landlady at 422 1/2 South Main.

He wore a dark suit and appeared to have little in common with men forced to stay in a flophouse.

He took no more than 13 steps when he walked from Room 5, where a 50-watt light bulb snapped off when he pulled a ceiling chain, to a dingy bathroom where he lay in wait to shoot Dr. King.

> 'I showed him Room 5 and he said, "This will be fine."'

His mission was accomplished at 6:01 P.M. . . .

He cut down Dr. King, standing alone on the balcony of the Lorraine Motel exactly 203 feet and 3 inches away across Mulberry Street.

He did not have the 30-caliber pump action Remington rifle and telescopic sight with him when he checked into the rooming house about 3:15 P.M.

"A Clean, Neat Man"

Mrs. Bessie Brewer [the landlady] said she left the inside chain latched on when the assassin knocked at the office door.

"He was a clean, neat man," she said. "I unlatched the door and I showed him Room 8, a $10-a-week kitchenette, but he said, 'I only want a sleeping room.'

"I showed him Room 5 and he said, 'This will be fine.'

"We went back to the office.

"He said his name was John Willard and I wrote out a receipt. He paid with a $20 bill. He reached into his right pants pocket, pulled it out and unfolded it with both hands."

(Police investigators took the receipt carbon and the $20 to headquarters.)

Mrs. Brewer said the man was as tall as her husband—about six feet.

B.L. Reeves, a 74-year-old retired hotel clerk, watched the man as he talked to Mrs. Brewer.

"I seen him when she checked him in. He had his back to me, but I judge he was about 5 feet, 11. He had dark hair and a pretty neat hair cut, about like yours."

Charlie Q. Stephens, in Room 6—between the room taken by Willard, probably an alias, and the bathroom—got a better look.

He saw the assassin when Mrs. Brewer was showing him Room 5.

"He was clean shaven and had a long, sharp nose. He had normal eyes and a square chin, thick hair at the front and receded on each side.

"He was wearing a black—solid-color—dress suit, a white shirt and a very dark or black narrow tie. He combed his hair straight back."

Mr. Stephens is a heavy equipment operator who was forced by tuberculosis to retire in 1954.

Mrs. Brewer said his features didn't register too much with her but his neatness was noticeable.

"He spoke like any other Memphian," she said. She said she never asks questions.

After the Shooting

Room 4 is rented by Willie Anchulz, who works for Du-vall Transfer Co. Frank Brewer, husband of the landlady, said Mr. Anchulz saw the killer immediately after the shooting.

"He said he saw him running downstairs carrying something wrapped."

Mr. Anchulz could not be reached yesterday.

Mr. Stephens said he heard the shot.

"I was in there (the kitchen) working on my radio. When that explosion went off it sounded like a German 88 [a World War II anti-aircraft gun]. I went to the door and walked out into the hall. I could see the man at the

Photo on following page: A neighbor of the Lorraine Motel shows the view the killer had of King's room. (Associated Press.)

offset in the hall. He had in his hand something wrapped in a newspaper."

The killer climbed a flight of 25 steps to reach the rooming house office on the second floor at 422 1/2 South Main. He fled by going down 20 steps at 418 1/2 South Main. The 16 units are connected by a walkway.

His actions between 3:15 P.M. and 6:01 [P.M.] when he squeezed off the fatal shot while standing on the bathtub and propped against the window shelf are cloudy.

He never lay down on the bed. There is evidence he sat on the edge of it for sometime. He also moved around the room, which has a well-wardrobe and a single window with yellow and green curtains in a flowered design. The curtains had been lain on the top of a nearby mantle, possibly to avoid obstructing his view.

From the window, there is a clear view of Room 306 at the Lorraine Motel. It was Dr. King's room. But the window is at such an angle that it would be difficult to shoot out of it.

The assassin, perhaps 30 years old, apparently sat there in a chair and watched the Lorraine Motel through binoculars.

Between 3:15 P.M. and 5 P.M. the killer apparently left the room, went down to Main Street and came back with the weapon. No one recalls seeing him during this time.

Mr. Stephens said around [unreadable number] P.M. the assassin went to the bathroom and stayed about 25 minutes.

> Some aspects of the situation read like a page that could have been written by Lee Oswald, the assassin of President Kennedy.

"Willie Anchulz—the man in No. 4—tried to get in the bath and then knocked on my door, I told him that was the man who had rented No. 5. He (Anchultz) returned to his room."

There was bright sunshine at 6:01—24 minutes before sunset—when the killer fired the rifle. Dr. King had stepped out of his $13-a-day room (for two) to "get a breath of air."

The second floor bathroom window holds a commanding view of the Lorraine Motel at 406 Mulberry. Some aspects of the situation read like a page that could have been written by Lee Oswald, the assassin of President [John F.] Kennedy [shot in 1963]. . . .

There also is evidence that the killer walked away from his crime instead of running.

"I got a glimpse of him going away after he dropped the rifle in front of my place," said Guy W. Canipe, part owner of an amusements firm.

"He didn't seem to be running."

Mr. Canipe said he walked south on Main.

A suspicious white Mustang with no front license plate was parked to the north in front of Jim's Grill. If the killer left in that vehicle, he had to retrace his steps somewhere.

Lloyd Jowers, owner of the grill, said he noticed the Mustang had pulled away at 6:15 P.M.

"I didn't see who drove it away."

One Assassin

If Dr. King had looked up and to the west of the balcony outside his room—Room 306—he could easily have seen his assassin.

He was looking down and talking to friends in the courtyard below when struck.

Small splotches of blood remained on the concrete walkway yesterday. There were a few red spots on the ceiling where a loose light fixture swung in the breeze.

In Dr. King's room, a large Lay's potato chip sack lay on the desk dresser. Two crumpled True cigarettes lay in an ash tray.

Dr. Ralph Abernathy slept in the room after the slaying.

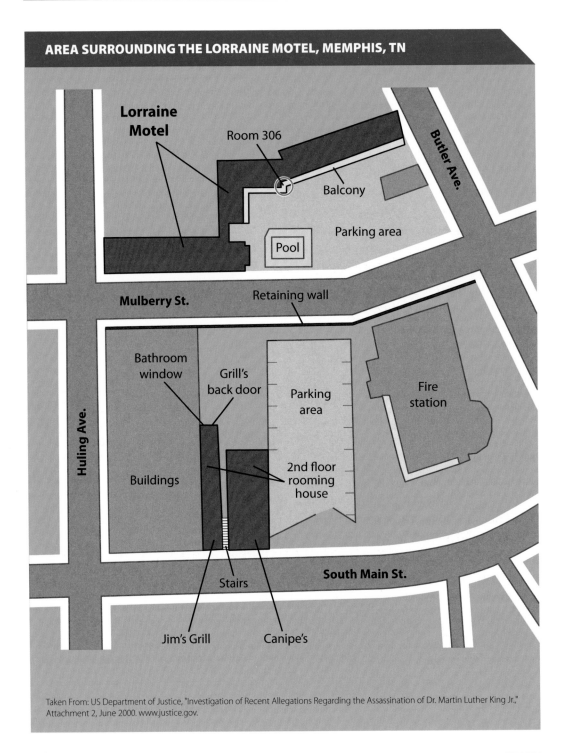

AREA SURROUNDING THE LORRAINE MOTEL, MEMPHIS, TN

Lorraine Motel

Room 306

Balcony

Butler Ave.

Parking area

Pool

Mulberry St.

Retaining wall

Bathroom window

Grill's back door

Parking area

Fire station

Huling Ave.

Buildings

2nd floor rooming house

Stairs

South Main St.

Jim's Grill

Canipe's

Taken From: US Department of Justice, "Investigation of Recent Allegations Regarding the Assassination of Dr. Martin Luther King Jr.," Attachment 2, June 2000. www.justice.gov.

Yesterday morning newsmen and others stood on the motel balcony and looked at the bathroom window in the brick structure up on the hill. It was still open.

> The assassin . . . seems to have carelessly left behind many clues—fingerprints, the rifle and other items.

The bathroom had been dusted heavily for prints. A black palm stood out on the wall above the tub.

A sign on the inside of the bathroom door said anyone "caught entering loitering in the bathroom hall" would be arrested.

While the assassin obviously knew where Dr. King was staying and concealed himself to shoot the civil rights leader, he seems to have carelessly left behind many clues—fingerprints, the rifle and other items.

Most of [the] evidence was being studied in Federal Bureau of Investigation laboratories early yesterday morning.

Attorney General Ramsay Clark, who flew to Memphis, told a crowded news conference yesterday afternoon, "I am confident that effort will result in early capture."

Mr. Clark said there was no conspiracy.

The assassin seems to be one man. The arrest of "John Willard" should wrap it up.

There were indications his real name [later discovered to be James Earl Ray] may be known to authorities already.

Riots Break Out in the Wake of the Assassination

Baltimore Sun

The *Baltimore Sun* is one of the major daily newspapers in Baltimore, Maryland. The following newspaper article, published three days after King's assassination, details the riots taking place in Baltimore. The violence included arson, gunfire, and widespread looting, and injured more than sixty people. The National Guard was called in and a curfew declared.

Governor [of Maryland Spiro] Agnew ordered the National Guard into Baltimore last night to quash rioting which broke out in the Gay street ghetto area about 5:30 P.M. [April 6, 1968], and which city police declared out of control within five hours.

SOURCE. "City Curfew Imposed; Agnew Sends Troops as Unrest Spreads," *Baltimore Sun*, April 7, 1968. Reproduced by permission.

Fires and Injuries

At the request of [Baltimore] Mayor [Thomas L.J.] D'Alesandro, the Governor declared a complete curfew in the city between 11 P.M. yesterday [April 6] and 6 A.M. today. Some 6,000 National Guard troops were available for duty in the city.

Two persons, one white and one Negro, were reported burned to death in one blaze at Federal and Chester streets. Nearby, the most serious fire of the night erupted on the northwest corner of Harford avenue and Federal street, consuming a dry cleaning establishment, a candy factory and another smaller building.

> At least 60 persons were injured. . . . Nine had gunshot wounds. Ten policemen were also hurt, none of them seriously.

At least one man, a Negro in his 30's, was shot and killed. Officials at the Johns Hopkins Hospital said he had no identification papers. He was shot in a tavern at Harford and Lafayette avenues.

At least 60 persons were injured, and most of them were being treated at the Hopkins. Nine had gunshot wounds. Ten policemen were also hurt, none of them seriously.

By 11 P.M., police had arrested more than 100 persons. At Eastern district, there were a total of 62 arrests. The Central district police station reported more than 30 arrests.

When the National Guard was ordered in, Maj. Gen. George M. Gelston, the State adjutant general, was placed in command of all law enforcement in the city.

Troops moved out of the Fifth Regiment Armory on trucks at 11:15 P.M. Each soldier carried a rifle—with a bared bayonet.

The rifles were unloaded, but each man had two clips of ammunition on his lapel. Each clip contained ten bullets. Every National Guardsman was equipped with a canister of tear gas.

Included in the curfew order was another order banning the sale of alcoholic beverages. Sales of gasoline and other flammables in containers was prohibited. So was the sale of firearms.

Among those arrested was Walter H. Lively, the 25-year-old head of the Baltimore Urban Coalition and a worker for the Union for Jobs or Income Now. Police at Central district said he was being held for investigation of arson.

All off-duty policemen in the city were ordered to report for duty about 6:50 P.M. Police officials said later they had between 1,200 and 1,500 officers in the East Baltimore area.

In the chief area of rioting—bounded generally by Greenmount avenue, North avenue, Chester street and Baltimore street—violence, looting and fires were widespread.

The National Guard Is Called In

At 11:30 P.M., Chief John J. Killen of the city Fire Department said that there had been 250 fire alarms called in since about 5:30 P.M.

In several areas, fires began and continued burning because firemen were unable to get to the scene because equipment was fired up elsewhere. There were several reports of firemen being shot at.

The violence appeared to be concentrated to the East Baltimore area, but there were separate reports of fires, looting and gangs on the streets in other parts of the city.

After 11:15 P.M., when the National Guard moved in, city officials said that things appeared to be quieting down. . . .

At 3 P.M., Governor Agnew, who had been in close contact throughout the day with police and National Guard officials, used his new powers to proclaim a state of emergency in Baltimore.

At the same time, National Guard Headquarters in the 5th Regiment Armory issued the code words "Scramble Oscar," ordering every one of Maryland's 8,000 guardsmen to their armories.

Brig. Gen. William Ogletree, deputy adjutant general, said that 5,000 men could be moved into the city in short order.

National Guard troops were deployed in major US cities to quell unrest after King's murder. (Getty Images.)

The Governor's proclamation meant that the State Police force, which had been on standby duty for twelve hours, could come into the city and operate under orders of the police commissioner, Donald D. Pomerleau. . . . Maj. Gen. George M. Gelston, adjutant general of Maryland, would automatically take command of all law enforcement officers.

> "Windows were shattered . . . and teenagers were seen running from the store with clothes wrapped in plastic bags."

But at 9:15 P.M., a spokesman for Governor Agnew said that city officials had just reported to him that they had "the situation well in hand."

The spokesman added that those officials asked Mr. Agnew to stress that his proclamation was issued as a "precautionary measure" only.

The disturbance began in the 400 block [of] North Gay street shortly after 5 P.M. The police switchboard was loaded with reports of windows being broken.

At 5:40 P.M., all Tactical Squad police in the Central District were ordered into the area. They were joined by other officers wearing visored helmets and carrying long night sticks.

Several groups made up primarily of teenagers were seen in the area, moving in different directions and under apparent leaderships.

At 11 P.M., the Mayor went on citywide television to appeal to citizens to observe the curfew.

He said that he was "satisfied" that the acts which triggered the series of disturbances last night were "spontaneous," but added: "However, these spontaneous acts were supplemented by some obviously planned attempts to cause trouble."

He insisted that the night's troubles had "not reached proportions identified as a 'riot.'"

Just before 6 P.M., first reports of the rioting came in from the Sun Cleaners at Gay and Monument streets.

Windows were shattered there, and teenagers were seen running from the store with clothes wrapped in plastic bags.

Police moved quickly to seal off Gay street from the 400 block north to the 700 block. No one was allowed to enter the area. Side streets were blocked off by police.

Fire was first reported at the Ideal Furniture Company in the 700 block [of] North Gay street about 6:15 P.M. It was quickly put out.

At about 6:30 P.M., another fire started at the Lewis Furniture Company a few doors away in the same block. It rose to two alarms by 6:40 P.M.

It was the last fire reported in the area, however, as the intent of those on the street seemed to turn to looting and breaking of windows along Gay street and in commercial areas running off it.

> 'Half of the young people seem to want to go home, and the other half seem to be having the time of their lives.'

About 7:15 P.M., the Economy Store, an appliance and furniture firm in the 900 block [of] North Gay street, was broken into by a crowd of about 30 youths.

Iron grating protecting the front windows of the store was ripped off, windows were broken and individuals moved into the store. One youth wearing an orange shirt was seen carrying off a small color television set. A woman took a matched pair of lamps.

Police arrived about five minutes later and the crowd scattered.

One plainclothes officer standing near the Belair Market, at the south end of the area of violence, observed wryly about 7 P.M., "At this point, it's pretty festive."

Witnesses in the Gay street area made the same observation. One called it a "carnival."

Shortly after 8 P.M. fire broke out in a tailor shop in the 2300 block of Greenmount avenue. While it was blazing, big bundles of clothing were dumped into the street, where a gathering crowd calmly picked through it as firemen were working unsuccessfully to save the shop.

David Glenn, a Negro who heads the Baltimore Community Relations Commission, described the atmosphere as strange.

The Time of Their Lives

"Half of the young people seem to want to go home, and the other half seem to be having the time of their lives," [Glenn] said.

What became the worst fire of the night began at about 8:45 P.M. in the 1400 block [of] North Milton street, where an A. & P., food market, a ten cent store and two other small shops were ablaze.

By 9:20 P.M., the Fire Department had sent in a fourth alarm.

A crowd gathered to watch the fire and at times hampered firemen by throwing stones and bottles.

Police in all sections of the riot area were periodically pelted with stones and bottles. Police were met with jeers and oaths wherever they came upon crowds.

All off-duty city policemen were called to duty at 6:50 P.M.

In the riot area, police set up a command headquarters at the Belair Market.

Around 9 P.M., police officials said that "between 1,200 and 1,500 officers" were in the East Baltimore area alone. Working on orders from the command post, they responded to trouble calls in nine-man teams using two cars.

About 9:30 P.M., police said they were setting up another command post at Park Circle, on the west side of the city, as a precautionary move.

They were only scattered incidents reported on the west side of the city, with nothing even approaching the scope of the trouble on the east side.

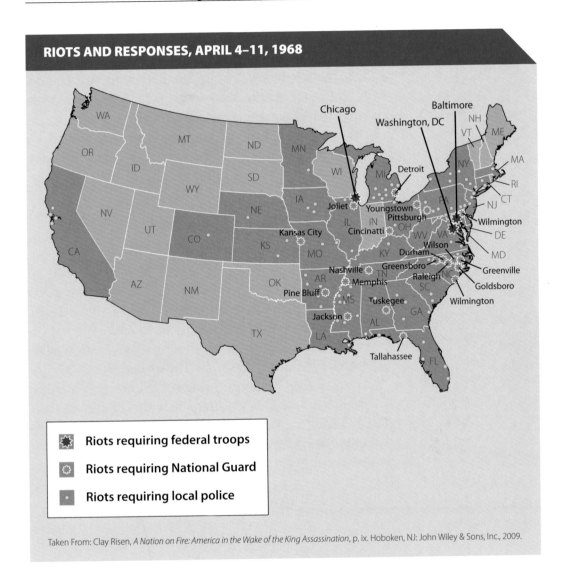

RIOTS AND RESPONSES, APRIL 4–11, 1968

Legend:

- ✹ Riots requiring federal troops
- ◉ Riots requiring National Guard
- · Riots requiring local police

Taken From: Clay Risen, *A Nation on Fire: America in the Wake of the King Assassination*, p. ix. Hoboken, NJ: John Wiley & Sons, Inc., 2009.

Just before 8 P.M., Major D'Alesandro reported to the communications center at police headquarters at Falls-way and Fayette street.

The headquarters building had the appearance of a fortress, with officers holding shotguns guarding each entrance.

About 9:20 P.M., police stopped a panel truck on Madison street near Greenmount avenue. They arrested seven persons in the truck, but said the remainder of about fifteen persons riding on it fled.

The truck, they said, was loaded with bricks and rocks. Police towed the truck away. About that time, they reported receiving seven calls in ten minutes.

One of those calls was for a fire in the 4700 block [of] Park Heights avenue, the first such call from the west side of town. It was not immediately clear whether the fire had any connection with rioting.

One of the major stores reported to have been looted about 8:45 P.M. was Levenson and Klein, a furniture firm, at Monument and Chester street.

It was about 40 minutes later that the first reports of trouble in the area around North and Greenmount areas were called in. The picture there was about the same as had been in the Gay street area.

Witnesses described Gay street, from Chase to Orleans streets, as one long "rock throwing gallery."

Large crowds lined both sides of the street, watching as youngsters looted store after store, smashing windows with abandon.

Elsewhere in East Baltimore: three stores on Greenmount avenue, from the 1900 block to the 2300 block, were burnt out by fire-bomb tossers; two more were burnt out in the 1200 block of Greenmount avenue; a major disturbance was reported going on in the Ashland avenue-Aisquith street area at 9:30 P.M.

> 'As far as I am concerned, this has nothing to do with the death of Martin Luther King. The man wouldn't have tolerated this for a minute.'

Bands of youths broke windows of businesses north of North avenue. About 10 P.M. six fires, all of them small, were seen burning within the space of several blocks.

Whenever a policeman appeared, the groups broke into loud singing—at [one] time "We Shall Overcome," the song of non-violence which became prominent in the South during civil rights demonstrations during the early 1960's.

Police asked for the National Guard to be called in when the unrest spread to an area too wide for them to contain it.

Maj. William Harris, a Negro who is head of the police department's community relations division, said at one point: "As far as I am concerned, this has nothing to do with the death of Martin Luther King. The man wouldn't have tolerated this for a minute."

CHAPTER 2

Controversies Surrounding the Assassination of Martin Luther King, Jr.

King's Assassination Inspired Numerous Conspiracy Theories

James Polk

James Polk is a journalist specializing in fraud, corruption, and espionage stories. He is a senior producer for CNN's *Special Assignment,* and is based in Atlanta. In the following viewpoint, Polk reports that, despite having been discredited, conspiracy theories about Martin Luther King's assassination remain prevalent forty years after his death. Many people have argued that the man convicted of King's murder, James Earl Ray, was not King's assassin. Some have argued that others helped Ray commit the murder, or that the FBI, CIA, or other government agencies were involved in the assassination or in a cover-up.

Photo on previous page: James Earl Ray confessed to King's shooting, but he soon recanted and thereafter maintained his innocence. (**Associated Press.**)

SOURCE. James Polk, "King Conspiracy Theories Still Thrive 40 Years Later," CNN.com, December 29, 2008. Reproduced by permission.

Even the FBI [Federal Bureau of Investigation] thought at first there must have been a conspiracy behind the murder of the Rev. Martin Luther King, Jr.

Even the FBI thought at first there must have been a conspiracy behind [King's] murder.

The name Harvey Lowmeyer was on the sales receipt for the high-powered .30-06 rifle left at the murder scene, John Willard rented the room across the street from King's motel, Eric Galt drove the white Mustang out of Memphis that night.

Then fingerprints showed all three names were aliases for the same man: James Earl Ray, a small-time criminal and Missouri prison escapee.

But 40 years later, conspiracy theories still thrive. A look at five of them:

Conspiracy Theory: The Man in the Bushes

Solomon Jones, the volunteer driver for King on his Memphis visits, told police that night he ran into the street after the shot was fired and saw a man running away in the brush opposite the motel.

"I could see a person in the thicket on the west side of Mulberry with his back to me, looked like he had a hood over his head," said Jones, now dead.

His account became the starting point for many of the conspiracy scenarios that followed.

Facts

All of King's closest aides interviewed by police said they saw no one in those bushes, which were directly below the second-floor rooming house where Ray was registered.

Among those witnesses: former U.N. Ambassador Andrew Young, attorney Chauncey Eskridge, the Rev.

Bernard Lee, and local minister Samuel "Billy" Kyles, who was the closest person to King on the balcony when he was killed. All looked and saw no one in the brush across the way.

U.S. Justice Department investigators later decided what Jones probably saw were nearby police officers rushing toward the scene.

Conspiracy Theory: The Second Gun

Loyd Jowers owned Jim's Grill, a bar located directly below the section of the rooming house where Ray was staying. Years later, Jowers would say a man came in the back door of his bar—from those bushes—and gave him a rifle to hide. He changed his story at least twice as to who that man was.

> Years later, Jowers would say a man came in the back door of his bar . . . and gave him a rifle to hide. He changed his story at least twice as to who that man was.

Ray's last lawyer, William Pepper, filed a civil lawsuit against Jowers on behalf of Dexter King, the civil rights leader's son, and in 1998 won a jury's verdict that there was indeed a conspiracy involving Jowers, but not Ray.

Facts

Jowers originally told police he "saw nothing unusual" that night. Police locked everyone inside the bar for three hours. No one could come or go. None of Jowers' customers said they saw anything out of the ordinary.

None of the prosecution's evidence was presented in the civil trial. Jowers, who has since died, did not take the stand. The only time he testified under oath, in an earlier case, he denied the story about a second gunman with a second rifle.

In fact, at one point, in a phone call to Memphis investigators, Jowers was tape-recorded saying, "There was no second rifle."

Conspiracy Theory: Military Spies and a Dramatic Photo

Pepper, the lawyer in the conspiracy case, said military intelligence agents had gone onto the roof of the fire station opposite the motel with cameras to spy on King and they captured a photo of the real killer.

"One of the guys, when the shot took place, took his camera and spanned it all the way around to the left, into the bushes, and he caught the shooter lowering the rifle. And he said it was not James Earl Ray."

However, Pepper never saw such a photo. He said he was told about it, tried to obtain it and was rebuffed.

Facts

Agents from the 111th Military Intelligence Group had been sent into Memphis after a protest march ended in violence the week before. Two of those agents did go onto the firehouse roof. Fire Capt. Carthel Weeden took them there.

But he said the agents decided the roof was too exposed. "If you're up there," Weeden said, "anybody can see you from across the street. They walked around just a minute and came back down."

In fact, Weeden told CNN, it was probably two days before the murder when the agents were on the roof. They definitely were not there when King was shot, he said—virtually eliminating any possibility such a photo could exist.

Conspiracy Theory: The CIA Connection

In the famous photo taken on the motel balcony with King's aides pointing in the direction from which the shot came, one man is not pointing, but instead is kneeling over King's body.

Unknown to the civil rights staff at the time, he was an undercover cop, assigned to infiltrate a black

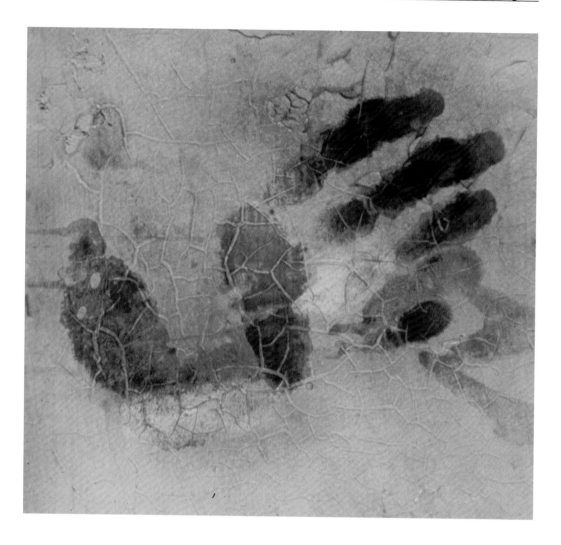

power youth group. His police supervisor said, "He had Dr. King's head in his lap. That's him holding him."

The FBI hid the fact the man was an undercover cop in the initial stages of its investigation. Later, the man would leave the Memphis police force and finish his career with the Central Intelligence Agency [CIA].

Fingerprint evidence implicated James Earl Ray in King's assassination but did little to discourage conspiracy theories. (Time & Life Pictures/Getty Images.)

Facts

The young black policeman was Marrell McCollough. He testified openly in the House Assassinations Com-

> "Ray insisted from the time he was caught that a mystery man named "Raoul" . . . duped him and framed him."

mittee hearings in 1978 and said he had run up on the balcony to attempt first aid.

The CIA said McCollough did not join the agency until 1974, six years after the assassination. His was a nonoperational job. He is retired.

A Justice Department report in 2000 said McCollough had passed a lie detector test clearing him of involvement in King's death.

Conspiracy Theory: The Mysterious "Raoul"

Ray insisted from the time he was caught that a mystery man named "Raoul," whom he met in a Montreal bar in the summer of '67, duped him and framed him.

Ray said it was Raoul who gave him the money to buy the white Mustang, Raoul who told him to buy the rifle, Raoul who told him to rent a room in the boarding house and Raoul who must have been upstairs there when the shot was fired.

Attorney Pepper said years later he located a "Raoul" whose photo Ray and others would identify—a retired autoworker in a New York City suburb.

Facts

In all the places Ray traveled leading up to the murder—Los Angeles, California; New Orleans, Louisiana; Birmingham, Alabama; Atlanta, Georgia; and Memphis—not a single witness has been found to place Ray with a mystery man.

The Justice Department cleared the autoworker in New York and said his daily employment records showed he could not have been with Ray in Memphis, Birmingham or other key places. Even Pepper conceded to CNN, "We never found anybody who placed James in Raoul's presence or Raoul in James' presence. We were never able to do that."

Most investigators have long considered "Raoul" to be a phantom of Ray's creation.

There Is Evidence of a Conspiracy to Kill Martin Luther King, Jr.

Mary Ferrell Foundation

The nonprofit Mary Ferrell Foundation (MFF) carries on the work of its namesake, an independent researcher of the assassination of President John F. Kennedy. In the following viewpoint, the MFF argues that the existence of so much contradictory evidence around the murder of Martin Luther King, Jr., suggests a conspiracy or a cover-up, perhaps involving government officials. The organization concludes that all records pertaining to the case should be made public so that the truth can be investigated.

The assassination of Dr. Martin Luther King, Jr. was one of the opening acts which plunged 1968 into a year of turmoil. Coming on the heels of the Tet Offensive[1] which showed the war in Vietnam to

SOURCE. Rex Bradford, "Martin Luther King Assassination," Mary Ferrell Foundation. Reproduced by permission.

be in disarray, and President [Lyndon] Johnson's decision not to seek re-election, King's assassination was itself soon followed by the murder of [Democratic presidential candidate] Robert Kennedy, violence at the Democratic National Convention, and a general unraveling of the country into a period of violence and despair.

> **Evidence of conspiracy was easily found, despite being ignored by government investigators.**

Like the other assassinations of the 1960s, the King murder had its "lone nut," in this case James Earl Ray, an escaped convict who purchased the rifle found near the assassination scene and was caught in flight two months later. But, also like the other assassinations, evidence of conspiracy was easily found, despite being ignored by government investigators.

The Assassination and the Capture

In the early evening of April 4, 1968, Martin Luther King, Jr. was killed by a single shot which struck his face and neck. He was standing on the balcony of the Lorraine Motel in Memphis, Tennessee, where he had come to lead a peaceful march in support of striking sanitation workers. About an hour later, he was pronounced dead at 7:05 P.M. at St. Joseph Hospital.

Shortly after the murder, a bundle was dropped near the door of Canipe's Amusement Co. near the assassination scene, and a white Mustang sped away. Memphis police officers found the bundle to contain a .30-06 rifle, ammunition, a pair of binoculars, and other items. The rifle had been purchased in Birmingham by a Harvey Lowmeyer, later determined to be one of several aliases used by Ray.

Pursuit of the white Mustang was thwarted by CB radio transmissions which described a high-speed chase between the occupants of a blue Pontiac and the white Mustang, and even describing gunplay between the ve-

The FBI vs. Martin Luther King, Jr.

The FBI [Federal Bureau of Investigation] installed at least 15 hidden microphones in hotel rooms Dr. [Martin Luther] King occupied. Arguing for the need for microphone coverage, the Chief of the FBI's Internal Security Section wrote that the FBI was "attempting" to obtain information about "the [private] activities of Dr. King and his associates" so that Dr. King could be "completely discredited." . . .

In November 1964, the FBI mailed a composite tape from the coverage of hotel rooms in Washington, D.C., San Francisco and Los Angeles to Dr. King. Included with the tape was a letter stating the tape would be released in 34 days and threatening "there is only one thing you can do to prevent this from happening." Those who read the letter interpreted it as inviting Dr. King to commit suicide.

SOURCE. *ACLU, "The Dangers of Domestic Spying By Federal Law Enforcement: A Case Study on FBI Surveillance of Dr. Martin Luther King," January 2002. www.aclu.org/files/FilesPDFs/mlkreport.pdf.*

hicles. These broadcasts appear to have been a hoax or diversion. The broadcaster of these CB radio transmissions has never been identified.

Authorities at first had little to go on. "Harvey Lowmeyer," the purchaser of the rifle found in the bundle, was described as a "white male, 36 years old, 5 feet, 8 inches tall, 150 to 160 pounds, black or dark brown hair," a description fitting many people. The FBI's [Federal Bureau of Investigation's] investigation soon focused on an Eric S. Galt, a name used on a registration card at the

New Rebel Motel in Memphis. On April 19, fingerprints on the rifle and other items were matched to James Earl Ray, a fugitive from the Missouri State Penitentiary. More than a month passed without Ray being located. Finally, on June 1 the Royal Canadian Mounted Police found a possible photographic match between Ray and a George Raymon Sneyd's Canadian passport. A week later, on June 8, Ray was arrested in Heathrow Airport in London, apparently on his way to Rhodesia [now the Republic of Zimbabwe].

Ray was extradited to the US to face trial. He replaced his first attorney, Arthur Hanes, with Percy Foreman. Foreman, who had represented more than 400 murder-case defendants, convinced Ray to plead guilty as the only way of avoiding the death penalty. On March 10, 1969, Ray pleaded guilty to first-degree murder and was sentenced to 99 years in prison. A "mini-trial" on that day settled few of the questions which had arisen during the preceding year. And Ray himself hinted at a conspiracy, interrupting the proceedings to say that while he "agreed to all these stipulations," he did not "exactly accept the theories of Mr. Clark (the Attorney General). . . . I mean on the conspiracy thing." Three days later, Ray recanted his plea and requested a new trial in two letters to [presiding] Judge [Preston] Battle. The judge did not act upon these letters, and was found dead at his desk of a heart attack three weeks later, literally with Ray's appeal under his body.

Evidence of Conspiracy

Since recanting his confession three days after giving it, James Earl Ray began claiming his innocence, saying that he did not know King was in Memphis and that his actions had for months been directed by a mysterious person named "Raoul." Beyond Ray's own possibly self-serving statements, though, there are several indications that there was more to the King murder than just

Ray. Among these are Ray's sophisticated use of aliases, evidence of framing, including a second white Mustang at the assassination scene and the convenient "bundle" of evidence implicating Ray, and several indications that Ray was aided or directed at times. For instance, Ray purchased a Winchester rifle and had it equipped with a scope, and then almost immediately called back and exchanged the rifle the following day for a Remington .30-06, telling the salesman that his "brother" had told him the Winchester was unsuitable. Ray had rejected a .30-06 during his original purchase as too expensive.

Researcher Philip Melanson has written that Ray used aliases which matched actual people living in Montreal, and began using those aliases before he first arrived there during his pre-assassination travels: "four of the five aliases used by Ray in the nine months preceding the crime were real Canadians who lived in close proximity to each other." These people—Eric S. Galt, Raymond George Sneyd, Paul E. Bridgeman—all lived within a couple of miles of each other in Toronto, and all looked very similar to Ray. Galt and Willard, another Toronto resident whose name Ray used, both had scars on the right side of their faces, as Ray did. Though Ray had used aliases throughout his criminal career, there is no evidence Ray had been to Toronto prior to fleeing there after the King murder, and no explanation for how he came to use these particular names.

> A petty criminal, Ray seems unlikely to have committed the crime purely out of racial hatred.

Other oddities written about by researchers of the case include a second white Mustang, not owned by Ray, which may have been the one seen fleeing the murder scene, as well as the CB radio "hoax" mentioned earlier, and a delivery of an envelope to Ray by a mysterious "fat man." Some writers have interpreted the evidence as a sophisticated operation which brought Ray into an assassination plot and then left him holding the bag at the scene of King's murder.

There was no eyewitness to the shooting, and there are credibility problems with the sole witness to Ray's allegedly fleeing the roominghouse bathroom from which he is said to have fired the rifle. The slug removed from King's body was never matched to Ray's rifle. The rifle shot was never proven to have come from the bathroom window, and may have come from the bushy area on the ground below.

Ray's skill with a rifle is dubious, and while he did commit armed robbery, he had never harmed anyone previously during his criminal endeavors. And the man whose career one author described as "a record of bungled and ludicrously inept robberies and burglaries" purportedly managed to kill King with one perfect shot and then elude authorities for longer than any other American political assassin.

Further . . . there appears to be no motive for Ray the loner to kill King. A petty criminal, Ray seems unlikely to have committed the crime purely out of racial hatred, and anecdotes of his racism are thin. The idea that he killed King in order to achieve notoriety is implausible given the lengths to which he went to avoid capture (nearly succeeding). As Ray's brother John told the *St. Louis Dispatch* following James' arrest: "If my brother did kill King he did it for a lot of money—he never did anything if it wasn't for money."

Skeptics point out that Ray's story of Raoul has never been backed up by any solid evidence, and despite some minor mysteries, concrete and credible evidence tying Ray to any conspiracy has never emerged. The problem here is that the FBI, which conducted much of the initial in-

> The House Select Committee on Assassinations . . . found a "likelihood" of a conspiracy.

Acts by FBI director J. Edgar Hoover (far right) regarding King put into question the agency's motivations in the case. (National Geographic/Getty Images.)

vestigations, was more interested in finding and then convicting Ray than in finding accomplices. The FBI had received death threats against King which it had never shared with the civil rights leader, and it withheld relevant files from later investigations. Beyond the FBI's initial investigation, the only large-scale study of the King murder was undertaken by the House Select Committee on Assassinations [HSCA]. And that body found a "likelihood" of a conspiracy.

The HSCA Investigation

The House Select Committee on Assassinations conducted investigations into the murders of both President

John F. Kennedy and Dr. Martin Luther King, Jr. In the King case, the HSCA wrote about the context of the murder, noting in particular the then-recent revelations of the FBI's COINTELPRO operations and its harassment of Dr. King.[2] Regarding the assassination itself, the HSCA interviewed Ray extensively, along with his brothers and many witnesses and officials. Some of the HSCA's findings were:

- Ray fired the shot that killed King, from the roominghouse bathroom window.

- Ray's "Raoul" story was "not worthy of belief, and may have been invented partly to cover for help received from his brothers John and Jerry."

- There was a "likelihood" of conspiracy. In particular, the HSCA focused on an alleged $50,000 bounty on King's life offered in St. Louis.

Some of these and other HSCA findings are on more solid ground than others. The otherwise-detailed HSCA Final Report is also silent on some issues, most glaringly Ray's sophisticated use of aliases. The alias issue was well-known to the Committee—in executive session [HSCA Deputy Chief Counsel, Robert] Lehner on one occasion noted that this "would indicate that a rather sophisticated operation was at work, and this would not fit in, as Mr. [Stewart Brett] McKinney [congressman from Connecticut] has stated, with the background of Ray as we know him. . . ."

The HSCA was also aware of a $100,000 bounty offer on Dr. King which was being offered by the White Knights of Mississippi. A number of post-assassination leads pointed to the possibility that members of the White Knights were involved in some fashion with the attack on Dr. King.

To what extent the HSCA investigated these and other issues, and what they found, is difficult to say at present.

There has been no MLK Records Act to match the 1992 JFK Records Act [which made records regarding the Kennedy Assassination publicly available], and thus the HSCA's files on the King investigation remain sealed to this day. The executive session statement quoted above is available by accident, as King-related discussion in these transcripts is typically blacked out.

The Civil Trial

Loyd Jowers, the owner of Jim's Grill located on the ground floor of the building which contained the roominghouse, confessed to involvement in the King assassination on ABC's *Prime Time Live* in 1993. Jowers said that a Mafia-associated Memphis produce dealer named Frank Liberto gave him $100,000 to hire a hitman to kill King. Jowers said he stored the actual assassination rifle in his restaurant, retrieving it from the real killer.

Ray's attorney William Pepper pursued this allegation, and the King family sued Jowers in a wrongful death lawsuit. This resulted in a civil trial in 1999. At the end of that trial, the Judge read the jury's verdict: "In answer to the question did Loyd Jowers participate in a conspiracy to do harm to Dr. Martin Luther King, your answer is yes. Do you also find that others, including governmental agencies, were parties to this conspiracy as alleged by the defendant? Your answer to that one is also yes. And the total amount of damages you find for the plaintiffs entitled to is one hundred dollars. Is that your verdict?" The jury replied: "Yes."

Perhaps the most remarkable thing about the King civil trial, coming on the heels of America's obsession with the O.J. Simpson trial [in which the football star was tried for and acquitted of murdering his wife], is that this event received almost no coverage in the US media.

In 2000, the Department of Justice [DOJ] investigated the Jowers allegation. Noting inconsistencies in his story, and calling it "the product of a carefully orchestrated promotional effort," the DOJ found the story to be "unsubstantiated."

Like the JFK assassination, the murder of Martin Luther King highlights the problems with federal investigations of such high-profile killings. Many believe that persons or elements of the government were themselves involved in each of these murders. Whether this is the case or not, it is clear that evidence of conspiracy has not always been pursued with vigor, and in some cases the term "coverup" is merited.

> It is high time for an MLK Records Act along the lines of the law which forced declassification of the JFK files.

In the JFK case, author Peter Dale Scott has written that government records tell us more about pre-assassination intelligence operations and post-assassination coverup than they do about the murder conspiracy itself, but "this oblique path to the truth about the murder is the best hope which the documents give us."

It is high time for an MLK Records Act along the lines of the law which forced declassification of the JFK files in the 1990s. The voluminous files of the HSCA remain sealed for no good reason. Those few files which mistakenly leaked out with the JFK files included the startlingly open discussion of Ray's aliases quoted above and copies of King "surveillance take" which made it into the hands of the CIA's [Central Intelligence Agency's] JMWAVE station [an intelligence gathering operation from 1961–1968]. There is likely more.

Notes

1. The Tet Offensive was a large-scale attack by North Vietnamese forces on the United States and its South Vietnamese allies. The attack was a failure overall, but showed that the North Vietnamese were stronger than had been thought.
2. COINTELPRO was the name of the FBI's counterintelligence program from 1956–1971. The program included surveillance of King, including wiretaps and threats.

James Earl Ray Fooled the King Family into Believing in His Innocence

David J. Garrow

David J. Garrow is an American historian and author of the book *Bearing the Cross: Martin Luther King, Jr. and the Southern Christian Leadership Conference*, which won the 1987 Pulitzer Prize for biography. In the following article from an online publication, Garrow argues that James Earl Ray is a con artist who has fooled the King family and others into believing he is innocent of murdering Martin Luther King despite the solid evidence against him.

SOURCE. David J. Garrow, "Triumphant in Death," *Salon*, April 28, 1998. Reproduced by permission.

Very few people mourned the death last Thursday [April 2008] of James Earl Ray, the assassin of Martin Luther King Jr. Ray's brother Jerry, who for years worked for convicted church-bomber and professional anti-Semite J.B. Stoner, was one of the few. But Jerry had reasons to be thankful, too. His brother had never implicated him—or their other brother John—in any discussions or arrangements that preceded King's April 4, 1968, murder. What's more, James Earl's notoriety had allowed Jerry to garner considerable public attention as his imprisoned brother's primary spokesman. Rarely did any of the eager journalists raise the matter of Jerry's long, intimate relationship with the once-infamous Stoner.

Outlandish Claims

But those who seemed to mourn Ray's death even more than Jerry were the widow and children of King himself. Coretta Scott King asserted that her family was "deeply saddened" by Ray's death, and proclaimed that it was "a tragedy not only for Mr. Ray and his family, but also for the entire nation."

Readers who recalled the awkwardly staged 1997 scene in which Dexter Scott King, King's younger son, shook Ray's very trigger hand and proclaimed the King family's belief in Ray's complete innocence should not have been shocked by Coretta King's peculiar expression of grief.

> "A bizarre susceptibility to outlandish claims of Ray's innocence has slowly spread throughout Martin Luther King's circle of aides and associates."

Coretta King declared that it was "regrettable that Mr. Ray was denied his day in court." King—or her press agent—had conveniently forgotten how Tennessee prosecutors in 1969 agreed to accept Ray's guilty plea, and forego a trial, only after receiving the King family's personal approval.

Since then, a bizarre susceptibility to outlandish claims of Ray's innocence has slowly spread throughout Martin Luther King's circle of aides and associates. The first to succumb was the mercurial and once-brilliant James Bevel, who began championing Ray in 1969 before moving on to subsequent alliances with Lyndon LaRouche [a political activist and convicted felon], Rev. Sun Myung Moon [founder and leader of the Unification Church] and Louis Farrakhan [leader of the Nation of Islam].

Next came James M. Lawson, the Methodist minister who had invited King to Memphis in the spring of 1968 to help rally support for a city sanitation workers' strike. Lawson became Ray's pastor, and officiated at Ray's in-prison wedding to a media sketch artist, Anna Sandhu, who likewise believed in Ray's innocence. The couple later divorced after an argument during which, Sandhu reports, Ray angrily declared that of course he had killed King.

The most prominent and recent recruit to Ray's side has been former United Nations Ambassador Andrew Young, whose credulity is perhaps the most puzzling and disappointing of all. Unfortunately, it has nothing to do with any actual search for the truth. Young and the Kings have never taken the time to familiarize themselves with the rich portrait of the Ray brothers and their vituperative racism that was provided in George McMillan's landmark 1976 biography, *The Making of an Assassin*, nor is it likely that any of them have sat down and read Gerald Posner's impressive new book on the King assassination, *Killing the Dream*.

More importantly, neither Dexter King nor his mother has ever responded to the repeated offers that Memphis prosecutors have made in recent months to come to Atlanta to brief the King family in detail about the prosecutors' latest review of the overwhelming evidence against Ray. What that review demonstrated was the extent to

which all of the supposedly "new" evidence cited by Ray's lawyer, William Pepper, amounts to nothing more than fabricated stories told by people motivated by the expectation of Hollywood movie riches and, in some instances, actual up-front cash payments.

William Pepper, James Earl Ray's attorney, persuaded the King family to publicly support a trial for the confessed killer. (**Getty Images.**)

William Pepper and Oliver Stone

Two figures loom over the way in which the Kings have succeeded in making themselves into national laughing-stocks. The first is Pepper, Ray's lawyer, whose outlandish claims of government involvement in King's slaying have been disproven and destroyed by both ABC News' *Turning Point* and CBS News' *48 Hours*. The Memphis district attorney's report highlights "the pervasive mention of monetary reward that key witnesses relied upon by Dr. Pepper refer to in their statements." In the current *Time* magazine, longtime civil rights journalist Jack E. White accurately characterizes Pepper as "either a credulous buffoon or a con artist." Most people who've seen Pepper's work up close would vote for the second.

The other figure is movie director Oliver Stone, whose forthcoming film, *Memphis*, will be made in partial cooperation with the King family. If Pepper is little more than a con artist, Stone more accurately fits into White's category of the "credulous buffoon." Granted a personal interview with the now-deceased Ray, Stone came away just as wowed as Dexter King: Ray "looks you in the eye and there's just an honesty to the look," Stone endearingly declared. Maybe we shouldn't be surprised, after *JFK* [a film written and directed by Stone that suggested John F. Kennedy's death had been a conspiracy], that Oliver Stone would be the last person in America capable of seeing through Ray's self-serving lies.

> 'They've got to blame someone else more important [than Ray], no matter what the evidence.'

In addition to the influence of Pepper and Stone, the King family is also motivated by a desire to remain in the public eye, and its embrace of the conspiracy theory certainly achieves that. But there is also something else, as one person close to the innermost circle for more than a generation hesitantly explains. "It's not rational," he says. "They've got to blame someone else more important [than Ray], no matter what the evidence." The unquenchable need to fill the lifelong gap left by King's murder has left them grasping at even the most outlandish claims, even at the price of destroying virtually all of their own individual credibility.

James Earl Ray's most successful crime was not his murder of Martin Luther King Jr., because for that crime

The Attraction of Conspiracy Theories

A conspiracy theory is likely to be politically populist, in that it usually claims to lay bare an action taken by a small power elite against the people. . . . By contrast, belief in the conspiracy makes you part of a genuinely heroic elite group who can see past the official version duplicated for the benefit of the lazy or inert mass of people by the powers that be. There will usually be an emphasis on the special quality of thought required to appreciate the existence of the conspiracy. . . . Those who cannot or will not see the truth are variously described as robots or, latterly, as sheeple—citizens who shuffle half awake through their conventional lives.

SOURCE. *David Aaronovitch, "Debunking Conspiracy Theories in 'Voodoo Histories,'" NPR Online, January 30, 2010. www.npr.org.*

he was imprisoned for life. No, Ray's most successful crime was the huge and grotesque historical scam that he triumphantly perpetrated upon the King family during the last year of his life. Having destroyed, irretrievably, the surviving family members' credibility, it remains to be seen whether King's own long-term legacy has also been harmed and diminished by the foolishness of his widow and children.

James Earl Ray no doubt was bemused by the King family's mourning of his fatal illness, but of one thing we can be absolutely sure: that Ray died a happy man. Not only has he gone down in history as the killer of one of America's greatest figures, but he also pulled off an even more unimaginable offense: convincing the victim's relatives to champion his own innocence and importance. No killer of historical import has ever come close.

There's much here to mourn, and none of it is for James Earl Ray.

King's Assassination and the Subsequent Riots Provided the Impetus for Civil Rights Legislation

Nick Kotz

Nick Kotz is a Pulitzer Prize-winning journalist, author, and historian. In the following viewpoint, he says that President Lyndon Johnson used the sentiment and the riots following King's death as an occasion to push through the Fair Housing Act, which was stalled in Congress. The act guaranteed that blacks would not be discriminated against in purchasing homes. Though the legislation did not address or remedy all ongoing racial disparities, it was another important legislative step for Johnson in trying to guarantee equality under the law for all.

SOURCE. Nick Kotz, "Chapter 14: Another Martyr," *Judgment Days: Lyndon Baines Johnson, Martin Luther King, Jr. and the Laws That Changed America.* New York: Houghton-Mifflin, 2005, pp. 415–421. Reproduced by permission.

P resident [Lyndon] Johnson was in the Oval Office when he received word that Martin Luther King had been shot. The president's evening schedule called for him to attend a Democratic Party dinner at the Washington Hilton Hotel, then fly to Hawaii to consult with American military commanders from Vietnam. For the first time, the North Vietnamese had agreed to peace talks.

Calm Amid the Riots

At 8:20 P.M., press secretary George Christian confirmed to the president that Dr. King was dead. Johnson canceled plans for the dinner and for the trip to Hawaii. Instead, he began to monitor reports of immediate and spontaneous rioting in cities around the country. He could hear fire engines racing to buildings already burning only blocks from the White House. Black America had erupted in rage and sorrow.

On the night of King's killing, Johnson acted with the same steely calm that he had summoned after John F. Kennedy's murder [in 1963, which resulted in Vice President Johnson becoming president]. He called Coretta King [Martin Luther King, Jr.'s widow] to express his and the nation's sorrow at her family's great loss. He dispatched Attorney General Ramsey Clark to Memphis with orders to bring the assassin to justice. With Defense Secretary [Clark M.] Clifford, he assessed the need for federal help as the rioting spread from city to city. And he quickly invited an array of the nation's most prominent black and white leaders to meet with him the next morning to reason together about how to restore a torn, divided America.

For Lyndon Johnson, there were somber memories. Less than five years earlier he had assumed the presi-

> Johnson quickly resolved on a course to honor a martyred hero—a lasting legislative memorial to the cause King had championed.

President Johnson pressed for the passage of legislation that honored King's memory and goals. (Getty Images.)

dency in the crisis of Kennedy's murder. Now, as he had on that earlier day of tragedy, Johnson sought to comfort the bereaved, to reassure and lead the nation. And, as in November 1963, Johnson quickly resolved on a course to honor a martyred hero—a lasting legislative memorial to the cause King had championed. The groundwork already was in place: it was to be open housing.

In 1966 in Chicago, Martin Luther King had fought to establish the rights of black Americans to escape their teeming inner-city ghettoes and live in neighborhoods of their own choosing. In Chicago, when King was stoned and his disciples attacked, the response was only silence. As in earlier battles, King's resolute nonviolent warriors had marched out of those ghettoes to face the ugly racism, anger, and fears of white Americans, cowering in the fortresses of their all-white neighborhoods. The American conscience had been stirred by black Americans walking for miles as they united to boycott the segregated buses of Montgomery. Deep feelings of compassion and justice were touched by the old black lady in Montgomery who proclaimed softly, "My feets is tired, but my soul is rested." The better nature of the republic's citizens had been stirred again by the peaceful march of 100,000 black and white Americans to hear Martin Luther King's dream of an America worthy of its founding ideals, and responded yet again to King's prayerful armies facing fire hoses in Birmingham and mounted vigilantes at the Edmund Pettus Bridge in Selma.

Now, as cities burned, as black Americans raged and wept, as his own presidency lay in ruins, its lustrous accomplishments tarnished by cruel fate and by America's unwillingness to respond generously to the least among its number, tormented by his own flagrant flaws, weaknesses, and doubts, Lyndon Johnson sought again to rouse the spirit of brotherhood in the land. Out of the ashes of King's death and of cities now in flames, Johnson would try to forge a final victory.

Getting Something Done

At 11 A.M. Friday morning, April 5, the president walked into the Cabinet Room, next to the Oval Office, to greet the cream of the nation's leadership, both old and new. Gathered there were Chief Justice Earl Warren, who had led his Court to strike down school desegregation; Mike

Mansfield, Hubert Humphrey, Everett Dirksen, and William McCulloch, who had led Congress to enact two epic civil rights acts; Whitney Young, Roy Wilkins, Clarence Mitchell, and Dorothy Height, who had steadily advanced the cause of justice from their venerable civil rights organizations. And there were the new leaders, including several who had been recognized and appointed to high office by Johnson himself: Supreme

> The most immediate action that Congress could take . . . was to pass the fair housing law.

Court associate justice Thurgood Marshall and federal district court judge Leon Higginbotham; Robert Weaver, secretary of the Department of Housing and Urban Development; Mayor Walter Washington of Washington, D.C.; King's SCLC [Southern Christian Leadership Conference] lieutenant Walter Fauntroy, vice chairman of the Washington City Council. As they met in the Cabinet Room, Mayor Washington informed the president that federal troops would be needed immediately to quell the riot in the streets outside. His police department had been overwhelmed. Firemen were under assault by rioters as they tried to fight blazes along Seventh Street, Fourteenth Street, and in north-east Washington. Johnson signed an order declaring martial law in the nation's capital.

The group then heard the young mayor of Gary, Indiana, Richard Hatcher, the first elected black mayor of a large American city, as he decried the still virulent racism of white America—racism further incited by inchoate black rage in the streets. President Johnson warned that society must not succumb to the violence that some blacks and whites now embraced to confront racial problems in America. If the prophets of violence prevailed, Johnson said, "that would be a catastrophe for the country." He asked the congressional leaders seated around the table to enact the legislation that he earlier had proposed to help root out racism in America. "It's been sitting too long in the Congress," he told them. Then President Johnson led these men and women to Washington National Cathedral, where they prayed together for the soul of the Reverend Martin Luther King Jr. and for the nation.

Back in the White House, the president summoned Joseph Califano, his director of legislation. "We've got to show the nation," said Johnson, speaking particularly of its grieving black population, "that we can get something done." With Califano at his side, Johnson wrote an urgent message to Speaker John McCormack and Minority Leader Gerald Ford: "Last night, America was shocked by a senseless act of violence. A man who devoted his life to the nonviolent achievement of rights that most Americans take for granted was killed by an assassin's bullet. This tragedy has caused all good men to look deeply into their hearts. When the Nation so urgently needs the healing balm of unity, a brutal wound on our conscience forces upon us all this question: What more can I do to achieve brotherhood and equality among all Americans?"

The most immediate action that Congress could take, the president wrote, was to pass the fair housing law [outlawing discrimination in the sale of housing to blacks], which still loomed in the House Rules Committee. "I urge the members of the House of Representatives to rise to this challenge," Johnson said. "In your hands lies the power to renew for all Americans the great promise of opportunity and justice under law. . . . The time for action is now."

Following the president's instructions, J. Edgar Hoover immediately directed the FBI to conduct a full investigation of the assassination. Their probe of the killing moved quickly. In an April 6 memo Hoover assured the president that "every effort is being made to identify the individual or individuals responsible for this murder." Hoover's daily reports to the president now focused on investigating King's assassination rather than on exposing King's associations and indiscretions.

The Dream Has Not Died

The president declared Sunday, April 7, a national day of mourning for Dr. King and issued a proclamation declaring that "the dream of Dr. Martin Luther King Jr. has not died with him. We must move with urgency, with resolve, and with new energy in the Congress, in the courts, in the White House—wherever there is leadership—until we do overcome."

Then Johnson set about the work at which he had always been a master—shepherding legislation through Congress. He told Barefoot Sanders (White House director of congressional relations) and Califano to enlist every available member of the White House staff to speak with members of Congress in behalf of the open housing bill. Where presidential influence might help, Johnson asked Sanders to give him the names of members to call.

Speaker McCormack immediately pledged his cooperation, but Ford was not swayed by the president's appeal. The House Republican leadership, influenced in part by the National Board of Realtors, remained opposed to accepting the strong Senate-approved open housing bill. A group of twenty-one moderate Republican House members, however, including the venerable William McCulloch, ranking Republican on the House Judiciary Committee, rebelled against their own leaders. Citing the "dastardly" murder of Dr. King, they called for immediate acceptance of the Senate bill. When the House Republicans caucused together three days later, McCulloch challenged his colleagues to remain the party of Abraham Lincoln.

> McCulloch challenged his [House Republican] colleagues to remain the party of Abraham Lincoln.

On Monday, April 8, as members of Congress returned from their Easter recess, [White House press secretary] George Christian went to the president's bedroom to report that rioting was subsiding, but not yet over, in more than one hundred cities. Washington, D.C., was still under martial law, with curfews being enforced by police and elite U.S. Army troops. The president had also ordered federal troops to nearby Baltimore, where rioting was still rampant. Christian shook his head over the violence: 46 dead and 2,600 injured, 21,000 arrested by week's end. The president replied, "What did you expect? I don't know why we're so surprised. When you put your foot on a man's neck and hold him down for three hundred years, and then you let him up, what's he going to do? He's going to knock your block off."

Later in the day, Barefoot Sanders reported to the president that the open housing bill was still in trouble in both the House Rules Committee and the full House of Representatives. He urged the president to call Hale Boggs, the House Democratic whip, or assistant majority leader, and former Republican House leader Charles Halleck, both of whom were still undecided about the critical vote.

With army troops now surrounding Capitol Hill, Speaker McCormack met in his office that afternoon with open housing advocates. "I'm not sure we are going to accomplish anything," McCormack began pessimistically. But he was willing to try. Gathered around the Speaker's conference table, Democratic House leaders and their allies from the White House and the Leadership Conference on Civil Rights read through the entire list of 435 House members. They needed to find another 15 to 20 votes. As they checked off names and made assignments, the officials looked out McCormack's tall office windows at the clouds of smoke still billowing from fires burning in downtown Washington. Sanders now hoped for a favorable vote from Jake Pickle, the Democrat who represented Lyndon Johnson's old congressional district; the White House had just approved a $1.4 million housing grant that Pickle wanted for his district. A leader had been slain, the nation's cities were in flames, but the give-and-take of Washington politics continued.

The Critical Vote

As the House Rules Committee met for its critical vote on Tuesday morning, April 9, the body of the Reverend Martin Luther King Jr. was borne on a farm wagon pulled by two prison mules on a four-mile journey from his father's Ebenezer Baptist Church to his alma mater, Morehouse College. Behind the wagon walked Dr. King's family and the fellow leaders of his movement. Following them came the politicians aspiring to the presidency— Vice President Humphrey, Senators Robert Kennedy and Eugene McCarthy, and former vice president Richard Nixon. In the cortege of fifty thousand walkers were lawmakers, athletes, entertainers, construction workers, milkmen, housekeepers, and one thousand black sanitation workers from Memphis for whose cause he had died fighting. At Morehouse, there were speeches. [Gospel singer] Mahalia Jackson sang "Precious Lord, Take My Hand"—the song King had requested seconds before the assassin's bullet brought him down. Finally, there was a mighty chorus of the movement's anthem, "We Shall Overcome."

In Washington, the Rules Committee was preparing to vote. Chairman William Colmer of Mississippi decried holding a vote in an atmosphere of riots. Fourteen committee members, divided equally for and against, remained firm in their votes of three weeks earlier. John Anderson, a Republican from Rockford, Illinois, cast the decisive vote. Switching from his earlier opposition, Anderson turned the 8–7 majority against the bill into an 8–7 majority in favor. This defeated Colmer's attempt to force a Joint House-Senate conference committee, with all its delays and uncertainties. The assassination of Dr. King had changed Anderson's position.

The full House of Representatives took up the bill the next day, April 10, 1968—six days after Dr. King's assassination. Expressing the sentiment of numerous colleagues, Congressman William Fitts Ryan, a New York Democrat, called on Congress to "respond to the Poor People's Campaign that [King] did not live to lead. We must pass the bill which is before us to guarantee open housing and the free exercise of civil rights. But that is a barest beginning."

> Remorse over King's assassination—and concern about the riots—contributed significantly to the bill's passage.

Other representatives reflected the attitudes of a still divided nation. William Tuck of Virginia argued that King's nonviolent direct-action protests were designed to incite violence. "Violence followed in [King's] wake wherever he went, North or South, until he himself fell a victim to violence."

At the conclusion of the debate, the House accepted the Senate's version of the legislation. On the critical vote, 152 Democrats and 77 Republicans supported open housing, while 89 Democrats and 106 Republicans were opposed. The final roll call vote, 250 to 172, was a formality. Remorse over King's assassination—and concern about the riots—contributed significantly to the bill's passage.

The 1968 Civil Rights Act

Despite the angry frenzy of rioters, the unending nightmare of Vietnam, and the derision of antiwar protesters, Lyndon Johnson had remained focused on the day-to-day business of a presidential and congressional democracy. In the first twenty-four hours after King was slain, Johnson decided that he would try to raise one momentous, passionate last hurrah for life's underdogs. He had announced that he would speak to the nation on Monday night, April 8. Perhaps, he thought, he could rouse the country again as he had done with his determined "And we *shall* overcome" challenge after Bloody Sunday in Selma [when peaceful demonstrators were attacked by riot police and Johnson had spoken out against the violence]. Humphrey, Califano, and others who had forged the shining moments with him urged Johnson to reach higher—to again inspire the nation to expand his War on Poverty far beyond its opening salvos. But Lyndon Johnson decided not to make that speech. He was too tired, too enmeshed in the Vietnam War, too consumed in coping with the petty tyrants of Congress, who would slash his beloved Great Society programs even further if he did not bend to their wishes. He was sadly but stolidly resigned to the political mathematics of the United States and its elected representatives. And they mirrored the voices of a divided people.

> 'The proudest moments of my Presidency . . . have been times such as this when I have signed into law the promises of a century.'

Civil rights leaders put the fair housing victory in sober perspective. King's successor as SCLC president, Ralph Abernathy, called the law "a step in the right direction" but said its provisions would be meaningless unless enforced. Whitney Young added his own historical context: "Those whites who feel that they have been purged of the national guilt and shame caused by Dr. King's assassination are dead wrong. The law is only one step toward a national resurgence of decency."

The day after House passage, one week after Dr. King's death, President Johnson signed the 1968 Civil Rights Act in the East Room of the White House.

"The proudest moments of my Presidency," Johnson said, "have been times such as this when I have signed into law the promises of a century. . . . With this bill, the voice of justice speaks again. It proclaims that fair housing for all—all human beings who live in this country—is now a part of the American way of life. We all know that the roots of injustice run deep. But violence cannot redress a solitary wrong, or remedy a single unfairness.

"I think we can take some heart that democracy's work is being done. In the Civil Rights Act of 1968, America does move forward and the bell of freedom rings a little louder. We have come some of the way, not near all of it. There is much yet to do."

Out of the sorrow of John F. Kennedy's assassination and the passion, determination, and skill of President Lyndon Baines Johnson and the Reverend Martin Luther King Jr. had emerged the 1964 Civil Rights Act. Out of courage and horror on the Edmund Pettus Bridge and in fiery protests throughout the nation, the two men had again ignited the nation's passion for justice in passing the 1965 Civil Rights Act. And out of the ashes of burning cities following Dr. King's assassination and Johnson's decision not to seek reelection had come one final declaration for justice written powerfully into the fabric of American law.

King's Assassination Hurt the Poor People's Campaign

Peter Ling

Peter Ling is a senior lecturer in American studies at the University of Nottingham, England. In the following viewpoint, he argues that the Poor People's Campaign faced many logistical and political problems. The riots after King's death eroded political support for change. The loss of King hurt the campaign further by robbing the movement of his charisma, connections, and strategic planning. The campaign's next president, Ralph David Abernathy, was not as strong a leader, and as a result the campaign ended in indecisiveness and disappointment.

B y the time [James Earl] Ray was apprehended [for King's assassination] on June 8 [1968], the United States was reeling from the assassination of [senator and presidential candidate] Robert Kennedy

SOURCE. Peter Ling, "Chapter 10: Going for broke: Memphis, 1968," *Martin Luther King, Jr.* Routledge 2002, pp. 297–301. Reproduced by permission.

by Sirhan Sirhan on June 5, and the PPC [Poor People's Campaign] that the SCLC [Southern Christian Leadership Conference] had launched in Washington in its efforts to be true to King's legacy was headed for disaster. In the weeks after King's murder [in April], African Americans had muted their criticisms of the PPC[1] and contributions to the SCLC had provided a budget in excess of $1 million. After two days of lobbying in Washington, Ralph Abernathy [King's succesor as leader of the SCLC] led a rally in Memphis to launch the PPC on May 2. The first contingents of protesters were expected to arrive in the capital by May 11 for a Mother's Day march of welfare recipients, led by Coretta King.

Opposition and Apathy

In sharp contrast to the liaison between government and the civil rights leadership that had largely nudged the 1963 March on Washington into position behind currently proposed legislation, the PPC leaders had little contact with liberal Senators and Congressmen. In Congress, reactionary lawmakers, warning of subversion and urging a clampdown, dominated the days leading up to the arrival of the poor. Criminally inclined black militants had already infiltrated the PPC, Senator John McClellan of Arkansas inaccurately warned on May 7, and from the planned shantytown on the Mall they would launch a concerted wave of looting, rioting and lawlessness.

> When aides proposed to President Johnson that he . . . call for increased social welfare expenditures, [he] dismissed the move as futile.

The violence that had rocked Washington and other cities in the wake of King's assassination was a more potent memory in the minds of the nation's senior politicians than any grief-sparked sympathy for the fallen SCLC leader's dream of a more equal and just society. When aides proposed to President

Johnson that he address Congress on the domestic crisis and call for increased social welfare expenditures, the tired Texan, a lame duck by his own admission, dismissed the move as futile. With an outraged "silent majority" fueling both the maverick campaign of [independent presidential candidate and segregationist] George Wallace and the political resurgence of Republican Richard Nixon, politicians with an eye on the November elections were considering whether action on law and order would placate their constituents' anger at inflation, a pending 10 percent tax hike, crime, and the interminable war in Vietnam. The Civil Rights Act of 1968, which some saw as a tribute to King, did extend federal protection to civil rights workers and outlaw blatant housing discrimination, but it also made the crossing of state lines with a view to fomenting unrest a federal offense and allocated fresh appropriations for riot control.

As Congress embodied the myth of the "outside agitator" into law, and prominent figures applauded Mayor Daley of Chicago's recent call for local police to shoot rioters, the political tide was still running against King's hopes of a radical program to redistribute power and resources. Even those within the White House who sympathized with the PPC, like [special assistant to the president] Joseph Califano, knew that in practice their goal was to soothe with words since there was little political scope for real concessions. Others, like Roger Wilkins of the CRS [federal Community Relations Service], could help to ensure that the PPC bus caravans arrived without mishap from across the country, but could do little to advance the purpose of their journey.

A Mismanaged Campaign

Getting its army of the poor to Washington was only the first phase of the SCLC's ambitious project, although it had consumed many of the planning meetings held while King was alive. What decisively destroyed the

Missteps by King's SCLC successor, Ralph David Abernathy, hindered the Poor People's Campaign in 1968. (Time & Life Pictures/Getty Images.)

project, however, was not King's absence, but the enormity of sustaining the Washington encampment for six increasingly desperate weeks. Attorney-General Ramsey Clark managed to block advance calls for the PPC to be banned, or for troops to be prepositioned around key federal buildings. When the SCLC applied for a camp-site permit in West Potomac Park between the Reflect-ing Pool and Independence Avenue, from the Lincoln Memorial to 17th street NW, Clark ensured that the National Park Service approved it. Like Chief [Laurie] Pritchett in Albany, Georgia [who thwarted protest goals with his restrained response], he realized that the gravest error would be overreaction.

In the aftermath of the assassination, the SCLC re-garded Clark's sympathetic response to the PPC as genu-inely helpful, even though it postponed the moment of confrontation that past campaigns had shown to be cru-cial in determining success or failure. On Monday May 13, with expensive media coverage, Abernathy officially opened "Resurrection City" by driving in the first nail for the A-frame wooden homes that were to be constructed in what he averred would be a model community of love and brotherhood. As a representation of the poverty that needed to be eliminated, however, Resurrection City could not be a utopia. Other errors followed. If the SCLC was to convey the city's radi-cal political significance effectively, it needed astute press management. Instead, it allowed the press corps to keep the community under round-the-clock surveillance and allowed its young camp marshals, often one-time gang members from Chicago or Memphis, to harass white reporters without regard for the media fall-out created. By the end of the first week, press coverage of the PPC was turning hostile, and Abernathy and other SCLC officials, such as Bernard LaFayette, had proved that they lacked King's press expertise and charisma.

> Press coverage of the PPC was turning hostile, and Abernathy and other SCLC officials . . . proved that they lacked King's press expertise and charisma.

The SCLC's schedule for the campaign had called for small-scale demonstrations building up to a mass rally on May 30—Solidarity Day. Like the 1963 March on Washington rally, this was planned to be a huge interracial gathering, with extensive middle-class involvement, that would promote the call for jobs and income. Unfortunately, Abernathy had become so fixated with the idea of his own great day on the Mall that, as progress on Resurrection City slowed, he first announced that Solidarity Day was postponed and then scaled down demonstrations in order to avoid trouble before the mass rally itself. This robbed the campaign of momentum and meant that there was too much time to focus on the mundane monotony of camp life. Compounding this mismanagement, the rains came on May 23 and continued for eleven out of the next fourteen days. Waterlogged conditions added greatly to the already overwhelming burden of running the tent city for the SCLC and seriously lowered the movement's morale. Whereas in other campaigns, King and his aides had refined their targets to generate confrontations and crises, the PPC remained quite literally bogged down.

Abernathy's Day

Eager to ensure that his Solidarity Day was worthy of comparison with King's "I Have a Dream" rally, Abernathy appointed Bayard Rustin, the logistical mastermind behind the 1963 march, to coordinate preparations. It was Rustin who insisted that Solidarity Day be postponed until June 19. But more importantly, he also tried to identify specific legislative goals for a campaign that currently demanded jobs, incomes, land, access to capital, and the empowerment of people within the government programs that affected them. To the anger of many in the PPC, on June 5 Rustin unilaterally issued a statement in effect scaling down the campaign's goals to the restoration of budget cutbacks in welfare, education, and employment imposed since 1967, a demonstrable commitment to full employment, the extension of collective bargaining rights to agricultural workers, and the passage of pending legislation on housing and urban development. This was a liberal reform agenda that no longer resonated with those who had listened to King's increasingly desperate demand for wholesale change. Denounced by his PPC colleagues, Rustin resigned on June 7. His departure increased the national media's hostile presentation of Resurrection City, a trend that the SCLC tried to mollify by approving a somewhat larger, though far from revolutionary, list of demands—many of them administrative actions to improve the delivery of existing food, jobs, health, education, welfare, and work programs—as the goals of the PPC on June 13.

Solidarity Day passed without serious incident on June 19. Underlining the implications of King's fateful choice of Ralph Abernathy as his successor, the speech that came closest to King's in power was delivered by Jesse Jackson [a key activist and King associate]. It could not equal King's cadences, but Jackson's reminder that Lincoln had freed African American slaves "into capitalism without capital" and that they now lived "in a land of surplus food with 10 million starving citizens" and "in a land in which some men swim in wealth while others drown in tears from broken promises, destroyed dreams and blasted hopes" captured the slain leader's spirit for the 50,000 crowd. When Jackson declared, "America can afford a job or an income for all men if she has the will to put healing programs over killing programs," few can doubt that King would have murmured: "Amen."

> Jackson declared, 'America can afford a job or an income for all men if she has the will to put healing programs over killing programs.'

In Resurrection City itself, the population was already falling by June 19. The majority of those who remained were young ghetto youths, who considered police-baiting a recreational activity. They added to the apprehension stirred by Abernathy's announcement of a fresh round of protests. Initially, efforts to expose the inequity of allowing bigoted local authorities to deny federal food surpluses to the hungry, while paying wealthy landowners, like Senator James Eastland of Mississippi, $13,000 a month *not* to grow food, seemed to generate positive comments. But these were quickly overshadowed by violent clashes outside the Supreme Court Building involving Hispanic and Native American demonstrators protesting judicial denial of communal land and fishing rights.

Too late, the SCLC adopted a direct action imperative that Jim Bevel [an SCLC field general] summed up as getting "Ralph's ass in jail." There were some chaotic clashes with local police on June 21, but no real pattern of protest emerged and Abernathy removed himself to the safety of a private Washington residence after death threats circulated. The permit for Resurrection City was set to expire on the evening of June 23, and the escalating problems of maintaining order and basic amenities encouraged the SCLC to abandon the site. Beginning at 10.00 a.m. on June 24, up to 2,000 police oversaw the dismantling of Resurrection City, which took little more than ninety minutes. It was a dispiriting occasion and, despite the fact that Abernathy and others were arrested as they tried to make one last protest at the capitol, it excited little positive media interest.

King's Assassination Provided a Window of Opportunity for the Poor People's Campaign

Gordon Keith Mantler

Gordon Keith Mantler is a historian. At the time of his death, Martin Luther King, Jr., had been working for economic justice with the Poor People's Campaign (PPC). In the following viewpoint, Mantler argues that King's assassination increased fundraising for the PPC and convinced many who had been skeptical to support the campaign.

When Kay Shannon first heard about [Martin Luther] King's death, she and her colleagues at the Washington office of the PPC [Poor People's Campaign, which King had been leading]

SOURCE. Gordon Keith Mantler, "Black Brown and Poor: Martin Luther King Jr., The Poor People's Campaign and Its Legacies," Duke University, 2008, pp. 146–157. Reproduced by permission.

thought it was a cruel joke. Informed by an anonymous caller, she only believed it after talking to an SCLC [Southern Christian Leadership Conference, which King also led] representative in Atlanta—sparking a mix of tears and resentment among the staff members present. "The girl next to me, who was black, started to cry and I put my arms around her because I was feeling the same way," Shannon recalled. "She turned to me and she saw that I was white and she immediately turned away, and I had this . . . ache because I knew that we were going to be confronted with that situation from then on." Indeed, Martin Luther King Jr.'s assassination threatened to disrupt whatever fragile alliances blacks and whites maintained, including those at the heart of the Poor People's Campaign. Of course, the mistrust and rage of African Americans toward whites was nothing new, and neither was the violence; King's death just compounded the problem. Every spring and summer had witnessed urban uprisings since Harlem in 1964—and the deaths, arrests, and property damage that inevitably came with them. Although less deadly, post-assassination disorders touched 100 cities, including supposedly "riotproof" Washington, D.C., and were the most violent uprisings to occur simultaneously during the 1960s. Yet often lost in the shadow of King's death and the subsequent violence was the Poor People's Campaign, the dynamics of which changed permanently with King's death. While scholars argue that his death doomed the campaign, the immediate response to the assassination suggests a more complicated outcome, even a window of opportunity.

Carrying on the Poor People's Campaign

Hours after the assassination, Ralph Abernathy [who would succeed King as leader of the SCLC] assured the press that "we are going to carry through on Dr. King's last great dream—the poor people's campaign," sparking a phenomenal outpouring of help to SCLC offices. "I noticed it a day or two after the assassination," recalled James Edward Peterson [a senior advisor to Abernathy]. "The phone started ringing; we were sort of barricaded in the switchboard room. Tear gas was being thrown around and the white people were being told that they could leave. . . . People started calling in, mostly black women in the suburbs." Kay Shannon echoed this memory: "[T]he phones started ringing and the black community started calling and saying, 'We want to help, we want to help.'"

To that point, many African Americans in the nation's capital had been wary of the campaign, driven by a combination of class politics, a fear of unrest, and skepticism of its success. To be sure, the campaign had some support in black Washington, ranging from prominent members of the Black United Front, such as Sterling Tucker and Julius Hobson, to faith leaders in the Interreligious Committee on Race Relations and the black D.C. Federation of Civic Organizations. Many other local black leaders, however, stood on the sidelines as white suburban liberals dominated early planning in the capital. Kay Shannon, who had been active in the peace movement through SANE [Committee for a SANE Nuclear Policy] and the United Nations Association, attended a packed meeting in mid-February at which she was surprised to see only two African Americans, one of them Tony Henry of the AFSC [American Friends Service Committee]. Even after they signed on, the sincerity of many of the local black middle class volunteers seemed questionable at best. They "always wanted their name to be on the program," recalled James Edward Peterson. "One particular person said, 'It's very important that my name appear on this paper, because it could mean a lot of money.' What he wanted to do was

> Fundraising for the campaign nationally became easier after King's death.

really to show his friends that, you know, he was joining an organization to help the poor."

Many such volunteers did prove more adept at supplying funds than anything else. Indeed, fundraising for the campaign nationally became easier after King's death, a fact to which the Reverend James Hargett could attest. A key SCLC contact in Los Angeles and a United Church of Christ pastor, Hargett said donations jumped in his heavily middle class black congregation and among Hollywood celebrities. Celebrities from television stars Robert Culp and Lorne Greene to Marlon Brando, Jack Lemmon, and Barbra Streisand opened their wallets—as well as their mouths—in support of the campaign, including a highly publicized benefit at the Hollywood Bowl. As SCLC officials had learned during past campaigns, it was important to take advantage of such moments; the Birmingham campaign in 1963, for example, had produced substantial financial support, but only for a few months. And the upsurge in fundraising proved well-timed, as SCLC records and FBI [Federal Bureau of Investigation] documents both demonstrate that King's organization suddenly did not have enough money to transport everyone to Washington who wanted to attend, especially from the West Coast. Yet, if fundraising improved, recruitment would progress even more—a development even predicted by [FBI director] J. Edgar Hoover.

> 'Everybody wanted to be a part of the Poor People's Campaign after Martin's death.'

Commitment Grows

Although some confusion ensued in places like Mobile, Alabama, over the future of the PPC, SCLC officials in April and early May witnessed an upsurge first in the attention to King—in death—and then personal commitments to the campaign. "Everybody wanted to be a

Photo on following page: On June 19, 1968—eleven weeks after King's death—Poor People's Campaign marchers packed the National Mall. (AFP/Getty Images.)

Ralph David Abernathy

In the long battle for civil rights, few leaders have had as an important a role as Ralph David Abernathy. From the late 1950s until 1968, Abernathy was the right-hand of Martin Luther King Jr. . . .

As a student in Atlanta, he had heard King preach in church. From there, they began a friendship that would shape both men's futures. In 1955, while both were pastors in Montgomery, Alabama, they began the first of many local protest actions against racial discrimination. They organized a boycott of city buses by black passengers that led to the successful desegregation of local bus lines one year later. To build on this triumph, the pastors called a meeting of black leaders from ten southern states in January 1957 at an Atlanta church. This meeting marked the founding of the SCLC [Southern Christian Leadership Conference], which was devoted to the goal of furthering civil rights throughout the south. King was appointed the group's president, Abernathy its secretary-treasurer. . . .

As opposition from individuals as well as government and law enforcement mounted, Abernathy continued to stress nonviolence. He said, "violence is the weapon of the weak and nonviolence is the weapon of the strong. It's the job of the state troopers to use mace on us. It's our job to keep marching. It's their job to put us in jail. It's our job to be in jail." . . .

Through sit-down strikes, marches, arrests and jailings, and frequently at great personal danger, King and Abernathy led a mass of nonviolent protesters across the south, working together to devise strategy and put it into action. The enactment of federal civil rights legislation in 1964 marked a major success. But tragedy followed with King's assassination in May 1968, after which Abernathy replaced him as SCLC president. He now added a new aggressiveness to the group's goals, notably organizing a week-long occupation of Potomac Park in Washington, D.C., by five thousand impoverished tent-dwellers in what was called the Poor People's Campaign. This effort to dramatize poverty was quickly crashed by federal law enforcement.

By the end of the 1960s, Abernathy's influence was in decline. . . . In 1977, Abernathy was forced from leadership of the SCLC amid a feud with King's widow, Coretta Scott King, and made an unsuccessful bid for Congress. . . . Politically and personally isolated, Abernathy died . . . of a heart attack on April 17, 1990, at the age of 64. In death, however, the criticism faded and was replaced by praise for his contributions to civil rights.

SOURCE. *Jeffrey Lehman and Shirelle Phelps, eds.* West's Encyclopedia of American Law. *vol. 1, 2nd ed., pp. 6–7.*

part of the Poor People's Campaign after Martin's death," said Andrew Young. "The funeral was the same way. We would have thought that ten, fifteen thousand people coming to Martin's funeral would have been all we could handle. There were probably closer to a hundred thousand people, and yet we made it." Chicano newspapers made rousing and poetic tributes to King, several ethnic Mexicans including [civil rights activist Rejes] Tijerina and [boxer and activist Rodolfo "Corky"] Gonzales were honored guests, and others such as Leo Nieto and José Gutiérrez, a fellow minister in Texas, even drove through the night—surviving a freak car accident with a bull—to witness the funeral procession. For Nieto, the hair-raising journey also cemented his commitment to the campaign.

In fact, grassroots activists of all kinds, many disdainful of the campaign just days before, reconsidered participating. This included so-called militants interested in armed self-defense. For example, Lauren Watson, a Black Panther from Denver, initially viewed the PPC's strategy as a waste of time—not because of its inclusion of other ethnic groups but its emphasis on non-violent protest. Watson, an organizer of the October 1967 anti-war march on the Pentagon, had teamed up with [Rodolfo] Corky Gonzales' Crusade [for Justice, a Chicano civil rights organization] numerous times to protest the war and police brutality in a city where the ethnic Mexican population dwarfed that of African Americans. However, he believed that non-violence as a strategy had run its course and had begun to embrace an "any means necessary" approach to social justice. Only after attending King's funeral did Watson change his mind on the campaign: "I . . . felt that as my personal tribute to Dr. King that I would go ahead and do it," said Watson, whose approximately 50-person organization also joined forces with Crusade members and more moderate labor and political leaders to march on the Colorado capitol and demand civil rights legislation in King's name. His participation did not mean he was confident that the campaign would succeed, he said, but "there's always room for (my) kind of thinking." Watson went on to take a leadership position in the campaign, using his extensive network among peace activists to recruit participants across the West, and then driving an SCLC car complete with radio-phone to guide the Western Caravan across the country.

Lauren Watson's about-face was not an anomaly. Although the biggest names in Black Power did not jump on the bandwagon—Stokely Carmichael, Floyd McKissick, and H. Rap Brown—many of their followers eventually signed on to the campaign. Members of the Black Panther Party were particularly well represented in caravans from the West, including San Francisco and Portland. Bobby Seale did not attend, but spearheaded a last-minute funding drive with local coordinator Sandra Davis to raise $10,000 for the San Francisco caravan. Milwaukee's NAACP Youth Council, which had become a leading radical voice for open housing, reconsidered advisor Father James Groppi's advice to join the campaign and voted to participate. Los Angeles' Black Congress, an umbrella organization for African American organizations in that city, endorsed the campaign and contributed troops. Perhaps most prominent was SCLC recruiters' success in convincing gang members from several cities not only to attend the campaign but also to serve productively as Resurrection City [the Washington PPC encampment] marshals—an internal police force of sorts. A significant number participated, including the Blackstone Rangers, Egyptian Cobras, and Disciples, all from the Southside of Chicago; and the Commandos from Milwaukee, affiliated with that city's NAACP Youth Council. Also agreeing to join were the Memphis Invaders and their leader, Charles Cabbage, who King before he died recognized as wanting to be included and respected more than anything else. These young men's participation immediately prompted both media and conservative attacks, but generally positive reviews from SCLC officials—who characterized the marshals as raw yet respectful and well-meaning—foreshadowing that organization's endorsement of Black Power in its August 1968 convention.

King's Death Muted Criticism

Even some of the campaign's loudest detractors tempered their criticism, even if they did not sign on to the campaign. Both Roy Wilkins and Bayard Rustin, vocal critics of King's plans in Washington, switched their positions after his death. Wilkins, who had called for the cancellation of the PPC just a day before the assassination, recognized the groundswell of support and eventually dropped his opposition; the NAACP in Washington offered its help with both legal assistance and the more mundane yet important contribution of office supplies. Meanwhile, Rustin offered to replicate his organization of a climactic rally at the Lincoln Memorial, as he had in 1963—an offer SCLC accepted. Several newspapers once critical of the PPC also reconsidered the campaign's wisdom and either offered tepid approval or at least refrained from criticism. In the immediate days afterward, the *Atlanta Constitution*'s editorial page, for instance, seemed to question its earlier condemnation "on the grounds that it could trigger violence. How mild that threat now seems in light of the disorders that have erupted in more than a hundred cities." Calling the campaign "inevitable . . . until Congress adopts an economic declaration of freedom," the *Constitution* declared that, "[j]obs, housing, a chance for dignity . . . are the goals now." The *Washington Post* came out in support of a march, but proposed changing

> Wilkins, who had called for the cancellation of the PPC just a day before the assassination . . . dropped his opposition.

its direction: "Let us have a march, by all means. But why not turn it around and have its route run from Washington to where the poverty is." Even the *Chicago Tribune's* editorial page, long a snap-tongued critic of King's plans, remained silent in the weeks after his death—as did the *New York Times* and the *Los Angeles Times*. Editorial writers at black newspapers maintained a wait-and-see attitude, offering low-key endorsements or remaining silent on the Washington campaign.

Congressional Indecision

Of course, critics remained, particularly within the institution largely in the campaign's bulls-eye, Congress. While some support for the PPC and its vision existed in both parties, such as Republican Senators Edward Brooke and Charles Percy and Democratic presidential candidates Robert Kennedy and Eugene McCarthy, the most vocal congressional critics were southern Democrats with poor civil rights records. Led by Senators Robert Byrd of West Virginia, Russell Long of Louisiana, and John McClellan of Arkansas, Senate proceedings became venues for attacks on the campaign, hitting a crescendo a few days before and after a vanguard of campaign representatives visited Congress. Inflammatory remarks by Byrd and Long, praising "shoot-to-kill" policies to quell demonstrators and looters that got out of hand, or charges of communist influence were commonplace. In an angry tirade on the Senate floor based on FBI intelligence, McClellan charged that "militant advocates of violence" would infiltrate the campaign, information based upon an informant deemed unreliable by the FBI.

Congressional committees also scheduled hearings on more than seventy-five bills designed to block the PPC. McClellan called one such hearing, in his Permanent Subcommittee on Investigations, in the hopes of denying the PPC its desired location for Resurrection City. To permit the tent city to rise on government property suggested official sanction of the shantytown as spectacle as well as the risk of disorder and "mob rule," opponents argued, and thus the issue of park permits became an on-going and central point of contention. But rather than re-ceive assurances from administration officials, including Attorney General Ramsey Clark and Interior Secretary Stewart Udall, that such denials would continue, McClel-lan faced equivocation. Instead of the desired hard-line message, the hearings ended amid a mood of uncertainty as Senator Carl Mundt questioned the committee's legiti-macy in setting security and permit rules and suggested that the Mall was the people's space. "I simply want to emphasize this because sometimes I get the idea that somehow or other we think that we are the custodians of this community, and it belongs to us and 'the public be damned,'" Mundt stated. "I don't think so at all. We are servants of the people. This is their home" too. Meanwhile, presidential aides boned up on Arthur Schlesinger's take on the 1932 Bonus Army march, in which Hoover and Congress looked obstinate. Concluded Matt Nimetz [aide to Presi-dent Lyndon Johnson], "We can learn from their mis-takes." In early May, the National Park Service approved a thirty-seven-day renewable permit for the PPC to set up a camp of up to 3,000 people in West Potomac Park.

> PPC officials realized . . . King's death ironically may have given the campaign a new, much improved lease on life.

Just as the striking sanitation workers discovered when public outcry over the assassination forced Mem-phis officials to negotiate a settlement favorable to the union, PPC officials realized Martin Luther King's death ironically may have given the campaign a new, much im-proved lease on life. Perhaps PPC organizers could parlay the massive goodwill created by King's death into an even larger victory for the nation's poor. At least momen-tarily, SCLC retained the ability both to raise substantial amounts of money and mobilize thousands of people for their cause. Yet linking these attributes coherently with grassroots strategies across the country remained a formidable test—even if many individuals had changed their minds and agreed to participate. Despite the real progress in reaching out to other minority groups in King's last days, SCLC still faced a series of obstacles, not the least among them the organization's penchant for high-handedness—or a peculiar form of paternalism. Thus, as Ralph Abernathy took the reins of SCLC and the PPC, trying to embrace new constituencies and build new alliances, King's grand vision challenged the way the organization handled itself as much as it challenged how the nation treated its most tread-upon citizens.

King's Dream Has Transformed America

America.gov

The following viewpoint from a US government website argues that, though much remains to be done, Martin Luther King's dream of an end to segregation and civil rights for black Americans has largely been accomplished in the forty years since his death.

I t was a march and a speech that the world cannot forget. [On] August 28, 1963, an estimated 250,000 people marched to the Lincoln Memorial in Washington, where they heard Martin Luther King Jr. give a speech of unsurpassable eloquence. Known ever since from its "I Have a Dream" passages, the speech gave impassioned voice to the demands of the U.S. civil rights movement—equal rights for all citizens, including those who were born black and brown.

SOURCE. "Martin Luther King's Dream of Racial Equality," America.gov, January 17, 2008. Reproduced by permission.

Transforming America

The speech particularly, coming near the close of the then largest demonstration in U.S. history, created a new spirit of hope across the land. It was one of those rare moments in history that changed a nation—paving the way for a transformation of American law and life.

> 'Righteous indignation against racial discrimination became widespread after the march.'

"It was a very peaceful day. A sea of white as well as black faces enveloped the Mall," recalls Dorothy Height, president emeritus of the National Council of Negro Women (NCNW). She was one of the march organizers and sat behind King on the platform. "I think it was a decisive moment not only in U.S. civil rights history, but also in American history. It resulted in a new determination to move toward equality, freedom and greater employment for people of color," she adds.

Height—still an activist and the author of a memoir, *Open Wide the Freedom Gates*—says, "The real significance of the march, and the speech, was that it changed attitudes. Righteous indignation against racial discrimination became widespread after the march. It led to a time so full of promise and achievement. You could feel it." Representative John Lewis (a Democrat from Georgia), the youngest speaker, at age 23 at the 1963 march, agrees. "Because of the march, because of the involvement of hundreds and thousands of ordinary citizens, we experienced what I like to call a nonviolent revolution under the rule or law—a revolution of values, a revolution of ideas."

The tangible manifestation of the change that Height and Lewis describe was quick in coming. Less than a year after the march, President Lyndon Johnson signed into law the 1964 Civil Rights Act, which banned discrimination in public facilities, such as hotels and restaurants, and also prohibited employment discrimination. The following year, the Voting Rights Act was enacted to ensure that African Americans had the right to vote in reality as well as on paper. In 1968, Congress passed the Fair Housing Act to remove discrimination in [the] buying and renting of housing. This landmark legislation was complemented by new policies, such as affirmative action, designed to counter the legacy of discrimination and to promote African American advancement.

The 1960s legislation is considered to be the crowning achievement of the civil rights movement. The Civil Rights Act swept away the more blatant forms of segregation and discrimination, banishing centuries-old indignities. The Voting Rights Act empowered millions of African Americans politically, leading to a surge in black officeholders.

The new laws took effect immediately. More evolutionary was a change in attitudes. In a 1963 *Newsweek* poll, 74 percent of whites said racial integration was "moving too fast," a viewpoint that seems shocking today when attitudes are very different. In a 2000 *New York Times* poll, for example, 93 percent of whites said they would vote for a qualified black presidential candidate. More than 60 percent approved of interracial marriage. And 80 percent said they did not care whether their neighbors were white or black.

The Dream Becomes Mainstream

If King were alive today, he likely would applaud the achievement of most of the aims of the 1963 march, while stressing that his dream still has not been fully realized, particularly as relates to equality of economic opportunity. It is a view also stressed by civil rights leaders, such as Height and Lewis. "We have made much of Dr. King's dream come true," says Lewis. But, he adds, "we still have a distance to go." Closing lingering economic and educational disparities among the races, however, is a much

Some see President Barack Obama's election as proof of a post-King shift in the attitudes of white US voters. (**Associated Press.**)

more complex task than ending legally sanctioned segregation and mandating voting rights.

As for King, his dream at the March on Washington is now part of the political mainstream, his birthday a national holiday during which Americans honor his ideas and his memory. Political leaders from both major parties supported a memorial to be built in his honor in the nation's capital alongside three giants of American history—Presidents Abraham Lincoln, Thomas Jefferson and Franklin Delano Roosevelt. It is a measure perhaps of how much a nation can grow and change that King's dream now is accepted as irrefutable truth by the overwhelming majority of Americans.

> It is a measure perhaps of how much a nation can grow and change that King's dream now is accepted as irrefutable truth by the overwhelming majority of Americans.

And not just Americans. Throughout his short life of just 39 years, King fought for racial justice everywhere, not just in the United States. To that end, he traveled the world proclaiming his vision of the "beloved community," and defining racism as a worldwide evil. "Among the moral imperatives of our time, we are challenged to work all over the world with unshakable determination to wipe out the last vestiges of racism," he remarked. "It is no mere American phenomenon. Its vicious grasp knows no national boundaries."

Even on the day of his "I Have a Dream" speech, when he was talking to Americans in particular, King was conscious of the worldwide impact of the march and its message. "As television beamed the image of this extraordinary gathering across the borders and oceans," he said, "everyone who believed in man's capacity to better himself had a moment of inspiration and confidence in the future of the human race."

The universal significance of the events of August 28, 1963, is underlined by Height. "Wherever I have been in the world these last 40 years, it's incredible to me how much people know about the civil rights movement and Dr. King—often in very specific detail. The world was watching us on that day," she says. "The march touched the world as well as America."

King's Dream Remains Unfulfilled

Svend White

Svend White is a writer and blogger pursuing a master's degree in Islamic Studies. In the following viewpoint, he argues that Martin Luther King, Jr., was a radical opponent of war, poverty, and racial injustice. The holiday in King's honor, White says, should be a time to reflect on our failures to live up to his teachings, not a time to congratulate ourselves. He concludes that, despite King's popularity and the holiday in his name, the United States has largely ignored King's most important message.

There's a refreshingly thought-provoking Associated Press item [in January 2008] on the Reverend Martin Luther King Jr. in connection with the holiday commemorating him and his critical legacy. I especially like how the article points out that, contrary

---

SOURCE. Svend White, "MLK's 'Dream,' Unrealized and Undigested," *Religion Dispatches*, January 23, 2008. Reproduced by permission.

to the comforting revisionism that reigns, King was not universally acclaimed and supported after his advent in American national consciousness, *even a decade after his legendary speech* [in 1963].

A Radical Social Critic

It's relatively well-known that elements in the government—especially [Federal Bureau of Investigation director] J. Edgar Hoover, who was convinced that he was a Communist plant—ignored the fact that by the end of his life he was a radical social critic who applied his vision to far more than race relations. As he began to apply his values holistically and across racial lines, he lost support among many erstwhile allies. Some of King's most important and heartfelt beliefs have gone done the memory hole, it seems. Deepti Hajela writes in the piece:

> "Everyone knows, even the smallest kid knows about Martin Luther King, [and] can say his most famous moment was that 'I have a dream speech,'" said Henry Louis Taylor Jr., professor of urban and regional planning at the University of Buffalo. "No one can go further than one sentence. All we know is that this guy had a dream, we don't know what that dream was."

Like the great prophets of the Hebrew Bible, the Reverend King was a human being and a leader whose vision evolved over time. Most critically for our current climate of intense government pressure on dissent and a largely domesticated Fourth Estate, King, like those prophets, spoke truth to power, and he did so without carefully circumscribing his message to politically safe areas of conflict.

Even if it meant losing some "mainstream" support. King was addressing a host of hot-button political

> It's both fascinating and depressing to consider how popular culture and even many of King's self-proclaimed political inheritors on the Left have systematically neutered King's legacy.

issues in addition to racism and segregation at the time of his untimely death. Hajela again:

> At the time of his death, King was working on anti-poverty and anti-war issues. He had spoken out against the Vietnam War in 1967, and was in Memphis in April 1968 in support of striking sanitation workers.

It's both fascinating and depressing to consider how popular culture and even many of King's self-proclaimed political inheritors on the Left have systematically neutered King's legacy by treating him as exclusively concerned with race relations. This despite the fact that by the end of his life, King saw and kindly proclaimed that all types of oppression and injustice spring from the same indifference to human dignity. Far from limiting his activism to racism, he spoke out with force and profundity about a wide range of pressing and controversial issues of his day.

Injustice Still Flourishes

The [blog] *Zeleza Post*'s discussion of King's mission and his legacy's subsequent commodification deserves to be quoted at length for its insight as well as eloquence. [In] "Remembering Martin Luther King: Beyond the Sanitization of a Dreamer":

> Dr. King represents America's enduring and unfulfilled quest to transcend these sins, to raise its low moral worth to match its enormous material wealth, both of which arose out the two original sins and their reproduction over the generations, to mend and heal the racial wounds of its sordid past. That is why Dr. King's message is often reduced to symbolic racial reconciliation, and his civil rights struggles are bled of the substantive demands for racial equality, namely, the need to address the distribution of economic resources and power. Lest we forget, it was economics that engendered slavery,

rather than racism as such, although following the fateful embrace of slavery and racism, economics and race worked inseparably to reproduce each other. . . .

Dr. King clearly understood that civil rights, antimilitarism, and the struggle against poverty were inseparable, that racism, imperialism, and inequality were each other's keepers, that civil freedoms at home were unsustainable with persistent poverty and wars of aggression abroad; that the Vietnam War drained resources that could be used to improve living standards for the poor, that civil and political rights (e.g. the right to vote), economic, social, and cultural rights (e.g. right to education, housing, and economic well being), and solidarity rights (e.g. the right to peace) were interrelated, interdependent, and indivisible. In today's human rights discourse, he would be regarded as a champion of a holistic conception of human rights, an advocate of social democracy, and a supporter of progressive internationalism.

Even accepting the dubious proposition that the systematic racism against which King battled is a thing of the past—tell that to young black men who get caught up in America's scandalously racialized justice system, with its draconian, life-ruining punishments for blacks for offenses that, when perpetrated by whites time and time again "happen" to draw light sentences—we're hardly out of the woods. The other socioeconomic problems Dr. King valiantly crusaded against are by most accounts alive and well.

It seems to me that given America's glaring gaps today in economic justice at home and principled, constructive involvement in the outside world, King's "dream" speech should if anything play as a stinging reminder of how *little* of his mission has been fulfilled. Instead, his stirring words are more often than not deployed not as a call for renewed introspection or commitment to equality, but

Photo on following page: A plaque marks the location of King's famous speech in Washington, D.C. Although King's famed words endure, efforts to fulfill his dream have dwindled. (Getty Images.)

as a self-congratulatory coda to America's modern social history that seems highly premature, not to mention fundamentally at odds with the message of the man and the holiday being celebrated. Like the self-satisfied Virginia Slims billboards of the past, in some respects we've come a long way, baby, but the fact that we've reduced Reverend King's holistic and unapologetically revolutionary message to the toothless, politically correct sermonizing of a Benetton commercial shows that his dream remains more than unfulfilled—it remains scandalously undigested.

CHAPTER 3

Personal Narratives

King's Wife Says His Life Was in Danger During His Last Year

Coretta Scott King

Coretta Scott King (1927–2006) was an author, activist, and civil rights leader, and the wife of Martin Luther King, Jr. The King family became convinced over time that James Earl Ray was not the sole assassin of Martin Luther King. In 1993 the King family filed a wrongful death civil lawsuit against Loyd Jowers, the owner of a restaurant near the motel where King was assassinated. Jowers had claimed that he was involved in a conspiracy involving the Mafia and the US government. William Pepper, the attorney for James Earl Ray, represented the King family. In this testimony from the trial, Coretta Scott King explains to Pepper that in the last year of his life, King had taken controversial positions that made him especially vulnerable. She says she believes the truth about his assassination has not come out.

Photo on previous page: Thousands crowded the National Mall on August 28, 1963, as King delivered his "I Have a Dream" speech. (Time & Life Pictures/Getty Images.)

SOURCE. Coretta Scott King, "Trial Transcript of the Martin Luther King Jr. Assassination Conspiracy Trial," Thekingcenter.org, November 16, 1999. Reproduced by permission.

Willliam Pepper: *Good morning, Mrs. King.*
       Coretta Scott King: Good morning.
       Thank you for being here. I realize how stressful it is at the time, particularly because of the gauntlet of the media out there. We're grateful for your presence. Could you just tell us by way of background what was the purpose of Dr. King's visit to Memphis, his involvement in Memphis and his coming here in 1968.

Martin came to Memphis to support the sanitation workers who were engaged in a strike for better wages and working conditions. He felt it was important to come to support them because they were working, poor people.

Dedicated to Non-violence

And how did the sanitation workers' strike and his support for that fit into the Poor People's March in Washington which had been planned for later on, the spring?

He felt that it was important that he give his support to them because they were a part of what he was really struggling to get the nation to understand, that people work full-time jobs but in a sense for part-time pay. Even people who were poor who worked could not make a decent living. So they would then be invited to join the mobilization for the campaign which was to be held in Washington.

> He dedicated his life to helping people to understand the philosophy of non-violence, which he [adopted] as a way of life.

Right. And was this support—his support for the sanitation workers in Memphis and the plans for the Poor People's March in Washington—to be covered by the umbrella of non-violence at all times?

Absolutely. He felt that—as you know, his whole life was dedicated to non-violent struggle. Any time there was violence of any kind, it was very disturbing to him, and he disavowed it completely and whenever he had an opportunity to. He dedicated his life to helping people to understand the philosophy of non-violence, which he lived it as a way of life. And so when he came to Memphis—I don't know, Counsel, should I mention that he—I don't want to get ahead of myself, but when he came to Memphis the first time and there was a march that he led which his organization had very little to do with planning, that broke out in violence. It was very, very upsetting to him because most of the marches, I would say all of them, that he had led had always been mobilized with the support of the National Southern Christian Leadership Conference staff. Therefore, they were aware of any problems, any controversies that might exist, conflicts between groups and among groups. But he came that day from a trip, got off the plane and went straight to the head of the march. Of course, the march did break out in violence. It was most disturbing to him. So when he—when this happened, he felt that it was very important for him to return to Memphis to lead a peaceful, non-violent march before he could go forth to Washington. He had to demonstrate that a non-violent march, a peaceful march, could take place in Memphis because of the criticisms that were being leveled at that time.

So he returned to Memphis that last time because of the violence that broke out on the march of March 28th, and he was determined, from what you are saying, to restore the position of non-violence to the movement?

Yes, that's correct.

Did he attribute—did he have any idea why that march on March 28th turned violent? Did he have any notion of what caused that?

Well, I think he became aware that there was a local— well, he thought at the time what was a local group of young people who really precipitated the violence. The feeling was that there were some forces behind them, that they were not just persons who decided that they would throw rocks and break windows.

King's widow, Coretta Scott King, acknowledged his awareness that "he could be killed at any time." (**Time & Life Pictures/Getty Images.**)

Vietnam

Now, what was behind or underlay his decision to come out against the war in Vietnam and to take on such a public political posture, if you will, which was quite a different change for him?

I must say that my husband had wanted to speak out against the war in Vietnam for many years before he actually did do so. He always—he understood the conflict that existed in Vietnam from its inception. And he realized that it was an unjust war in the first place. Then it was being fought against, you know, people of color who were poor. And wars, of course, for him didn't solve any social problems but created more problems than they solved.

He felt that this particular war was not—we could not win. Of course, history proved him right within a very short period of time after he spoke out. As a matter of fact, one year after he spoke out against the war, he was vindicated in that the nation had reversed itself and its policy toward that war.

That was April 4th, 1968, when he actually spoke out against the war in his first public statement. But he said he had to do it because his conscience—he could no longer live with his conscience without taking a position. He felt that [in] doing so, perhaps he could help to mobilize other public opinion in support of his position, which was, again, against the war.

Do you recall the reaction of other civil rights leaders at that time when he came out against the war?

Yes, I do. Civil rights leaders, other opinion makers, all criticized him, both black and white. It was certainly—certainly he expected it, but he probably didn't expect some of the people who criticized him to do so publicly. His way in the non-violent way was to privately disagree and to go and talk to persons which are having a disagreement, but to be attacked publicly was very difficult for him. He also knew that if he spoke out, it would probably affect the support, the financial support, for his organization, the Southern Christian Leadership Conference. And, of course, it did

> I remember him saying that because of the criticisms that he had gotten as he had spoken out against the war, the media had stopped carrying any of his statements.

very profoundly. He knew that before he took that risk and that position. So it wasn't surprising, but, nevertheless, it was painful.

Was there much discussion at the time about him running for public office because he was being pushed forward as a third-party candidate with Dr. Benjamin Spock as an alternative to Lyndon Johnson's being returned to office at that time? What do you recall about him moving in that direction of more serious political activity?

Well, I was aware of the fact that there was talk about his running for public office. It was interesting because from what I knew of him, I never thought that he would run for public office. Just knowing the kind of person he was, and because, you know, politics is very important and necessary, but he would be freer to make statements according to his conscience if he didn't run for public office, and because he was Christian minister and because he took his commitment so seriously, I felt that it would have been difficult for him. But at the same time I remember him saying that because of the criticisms that he had gotten as he had spoken out against the war, the media had stopped carrying any of his statements and they didn't understand—no one was getting his message, because the message wasn't being carried forth. There were a number of critical articles and some cover stories that were very critical of him at that time. *Time* magazine, for instance, did one in 1967 that was extremely critical. He had been the *Time* man of the year in 1964 after the [Nobel] Peace Prize, and 1967 was the first time, so it was, again, very painful for him not to be able to get his message out. So he said if [he] did run for office, it would be one way of getting [his] message out because [he] would have to be given equal time. The interesting thing about my husband, he always considered, you know, every aspect of an issue, both the pros and the cons. And then he would make his mind up as to what he would do.

Danger in Memphis

Were there any comments that he made the night before his departure to Memphis, that last trip, any indications that he had of potential danger or the seriousness of the task that he faced in Memphis?

I don't remember specific comments in that regard. But he had—after he returned from Memphis after the violence broke out, which was like on a Friday evening, he went back on a Tuesday—he went back on—

He arrived on a Wednesday, the 3rd.

—on Wednesday morning. But in between that time I was aware of how heavily it weighed on him, the problem of—this whole problem of the sanitation workers' conflict and what he could do to help by getting his staff united. Because some of the staff didn't feel he should go to Memphis in the first place. He was very strongly in favor of that.

So he came home late—I guess it was Tuesday evening he came in. There was not time to talk. He got up very early Wednesday morning to go to Memphis. He always called me, you know, almost every night when he was on trips, so he didn't say [a] whole lot about it, but I could tell that he had a lot of anxiety and it was very heavily weighing on his mind.

> Given the positions that he had taken, he realized that . . . he could be killed at any time.

Did he go through these times, and particularly this last year, manifesting an awareness that his life was in danger, that he had taken a path of action now that might have brought his life into danger?

Yes. I think he was aware of that certainly. I might say he was aware from the early days after Montgomery, Montgomery forward, but I think as he got closer toward this period of his life, he was even more acutely aware. Given the positions that he had taken, he realized that, you know, he could be killed at any time, but for him, his commitment to what he believed and to a higher authority was such that he didn't mind giving his life for a cause that he believed in.

He used to say that the end of life is not to be happy but to do God's will, come what may. So for him being happy was when he could come out against the war against Vietnam. He said to a colleague, and I heard this on the telephone, I was the happiest man in the world when I could come out personally against this evil and immoral war, because I came to a point where I felt that silence was betrayal.

So that was—I think that was his position.

Seeking the Truth

Mrs. King, on March 10th, 1969, one James Earl Ray entered a guilty plea and was sentenced to ninety-nine years in prison for the assassination of your husband. Mr. Ray stayed in prison until he died. But he tried continually to get a trial. At one point the family decided to support an effort for a trial for Mr. Ray. Why did the family take that position that late in the day at that point in time?

Well, as a matter of fact, it was because . . . of new information that we had received and largely because of the efforts that you had put forth to investigate a number of these leads that had come out and found that they were reliable enough. When we looked at it and investigated it, we felt then that we had to take a position. For years we hoped that somebody else would find out, find the answers. We wanted to know the truth. But the truth was elusive.

We wanted to go on with our lives. We felt the only way we could do it was to really take the position that we did take, because the evidence pointed away from Mr. Ray, not that he might have not had some involvement but he was not the person we felt that really actually killed him. . . .

What was the general reaction to the family as a result of that position? Was there animosity? Were there attacks, lawsuits? What happened to the family, yourself and the children and the organization as a result of that position?

Well, there were a number of media articles that were negative toward the family. As a result of that—there were several really and over a period of months, and as a result of it, we feel that there was some—it had affected some of the support that we might have been able to receive for the King Center [the official memorial dedicated to the legacy of Martin Luther King].

Financial support?

Financial support, yes.

Contributions?

Yes.

Is that similar to what happened to SCLC back in 1967?

That's right.

Mrs. King, why is the family bringing this action now thirty—almost thirty-one years later against the defendant, Mr. [Loyd] Jowers [the owner of a restaurant near the place where King was killed]?

> If we know the truth, we can be free, and we can go on with our lives.

Well, it has only been recently that we realized the extent of Mr. Jowers' involvement. So we felt that it was important to bring it now. We're all getting older, I'll say, and, of course, we wanted to be able to get the truth, as much of it as we can, out before it gets later.

I don't know how much longer any of us will be around. That's not given. But the fact is that my family, my children and I—I've always felt that somehow the truth would be known, and I hoped that I would live to see it. And it is important I think for the sake of healing for so many people, my family, for other people, for the nation. I think Martin Luther King, Jr., served this nation. He was a servant. He gave his—he willingly gave his life if it was necessary. It is important to know, actually not because we feel a sense of revenge—we never have.

We have no feeling of bitterness or hatred toward anybody. But just the fact that if we know the truth, we can be free, and we can go on with our lives.

Mrs. King, is the family seeking a large monetary award from Mr. Jowers as a result of this action?

No, it is not about money. That's not the issue. I think what we're concerned about is the fact that certainly there is some liability by Mr. Jowers, but we're concerned about the truth, having the truth coming out, and in a court of law so that it can be documented for all. And we were hoping that this would be one way of getting to the truth.

A Presidential Candidate Asks People to Respond to King's Death with Love and Wisdom

Robert F. Kennedy

> Robert F. Kennedy (1925–1968) was a US attorney general and a Democratic senator from New York. At the time of King's assassination, he was running for president of the United States. He delivered the following speech at a campaign stop in Indianapolis before a mostly African American audience moments after he heard of King's death. In the speech, he asks his listeners to respond to the assassination not with hate and violence, but with love and patience.

SOURCE. Robert F. Kennedy, "On the Death of Martin Luther King," Historyplace.com, April 4, 1968. Reproduced by permission.

Ladies and Gentlemen—I'm only going to talk to you just for a minute or so this evening. Because . . . I have some very sad news for all of you, and I think sad news for all of our fellow citizens, and people who love peace all over the world, and that is that Martin Luther King was shot and was killed tonight in Memphis, Tennessee.

Martin Luther King dedicated his life to love and to justice between fellow human beings. He died in the cause of that effort. In this difficult day, in this difficult time for the United States, it's perhaps well to ask what kind of a nation we are and what direction we want to move in.

> We can make an effort, as Martin Luther King did, to understand and to comprehend, and replace that violence . . . with . . . compassion and love.

For those of you who are black—considering the evidence evidently is that there were white people who were responsible—you can be filled with bitterness, and with hatred, and a desire for revenge.

We can move in that direction as a country, in greater polarization—black people amongst blacks, and white amongst whites, filled with hatred toward one another. Or we can make an effort, as Martin Luther King did, to understand and to comprehend, and replace that violence, that stain of bloodshed that has spread across our land, with an effort to understand, compassion and love.

For those of you who are black and are tempted to be filled with hatred and mistrust of the injustice of such an act, against all white people, I would only say that I can also feel in my own heart the same kind of feeling. I had a member of my family killed, but he was killed by a white man. [President John F. Kennedy, Robert's brother, was assassinated in 1963.]

But we have to make an effort in the United States, we have to make an effort to understand, to get beyond these rather difficult times.

Many credit Robert F. Kennedy's April 4, 1968, speech with forestalling riots in Indianapolis after King's death. (Time & Life Pictures/Getty Images.)

My favorite poet was Aeschylus [an ancient Greek writer]. He once wrote: "Even in our sleep, pain which cannot forget falls drop by drop upon the heart, until, in our own despair, against our will, comes wisdom through the awful grace of God."

What we need in the United States is not division; what we need in the United States is not hatred; what we need in the United States is not violence and lawlessness, but is love and wisdom, and compassion toward one another, and a feeling of justice toward those who still suffer within our country, whether they be white or whether they be black.

So I ask you tonight to return home, to say a prayer for the family of Martin Luther King, yeah that's true, but more importantly to say a prayer for our own country, which all of us love—a prayer for understanding and that compassion of which I spoke. We can do well in this country. We will have difficult times. We've had difficult times in the past. And we will have difficult times in the future. It is not the end of violence; it is not the end of lawlessness; and it's not the end of disorder.

> Let us dedicate ourselves . . . to tame the savageness of man and make gentle the life of this world.

But the vast majority of white people and the vast majority of black people in this country want to live together, want to improve the quality of our life, and want justice for all human beings that abide in our land.

Let us dedicate ourselves to what the Greeks wrote so many years ago: to tame the savageness of man and make gentle the life of this world.

Let us dedicate ourselves to that, and say a prayer for our country and for our people. Thank you very much.

A Writer Remembers the Tragedy of King's Death

James Baldwin

James Baldwin (1924–1987) was a prominent gay African American writer and civil rights activist. In the following essay, he recounts hearing about the death of Martin Luther King, who was an acquaintance, and about attending King's funeral. He links his grief and shock to his memories of other assassinated civil rights activists, particularly Medgar Evers, who was a personal friend of Baldwin's, and to the assassination of Malcolm X, a black activist about whom Baldwin was writing a screenplay.

There is a day in Palm Springs that I will remember forever, a bright day. I had moved there from the Beverly Hills Hotel, into a house the producer had found for me. Billy Dee Williams [an actor] had come to town, and he was staying at the house; and a lot of

---

SOURCE. James Baldwin, "To Be Baptized," *No Name in the Street.* © 1972 by James Baldwin. Copyright renewed. Published by Vintage Books. Reproduced by arrangement with the James Baldwin Estate.

the day had been spent with a very bright, young, lady reporter, who was interviewing me about the film version of Malcolm [X's life, which Baldwin was working on]. I felt very confident that day—I was never to feel so confident again—and I talked very freely to the reporter. (Too freely, Marvin Worth, the producer, was to tell me later.) I had decided to lay my cards on the table and to state, as clearly as I could, what I felt the movie was about and how I intended to handle it. I thought that this might make things simpler later on, but I was wrong about that. The studio and I were at loggerheads, really, from the moment I stepped off the plane. Anyway, I had opted for candor, or a reasonable facsimile of same, and sounded as though I were in charge of the film, as, indeed, by my lights, for that moment, certainly, I had to be. I was really in a difficult position because, by both temperament and experience, I tend to work alone, and I dread making announcements concerning my work. But I was in a very public position, and I thought that I had better make my own announcements rather than have them made for me. The studio, on the other hand, did not want me making announcements of any kind at all. So there we were, and this particular tension, since it got to the bloody heart of the matter—the question of by whose vision, precisely, this film was to be controlled—was not to be resolved until I finally threw up my hands and walked away.

The Phone Call

I very much wanted Billy Dee for Malcolm, and since no one else had any other ideas, I didn't see why this couldn't work out. In brutal Hollywood terms, [actor Sidney] Poitier is the only really big, black box-office star, and this fact, especially since Marvin had asked me to "keep an eye out" for an actor, gave me, as I considered it, a free hand. To tell the bitter truth, from the very first days we discussed it, I had never had any intention of allowing the Columbia brass to cast this part: I was determined to take my name off the production if I were overruled. Call this bone-headed stupidity, or insufferable arrogance, or what you will—I had made my decision, and once I had made it, nothing could make me waver, and nothing could make me alter it. If there were errors in my concept of the film, and if I made errors in the execution, well, then, I would have to pay for my errors. But one can learn from one's errors. What one cannot survive is allowing other people to make your errors for you, discarding your own vision, in which, at least, you believe, for someone else's vision, in which you do *not* believe.

Anyway, all that s--- had yet to hit the fan. This day, the girl, and Billy, and I had a few drinks by the swimming pool. Walter, my cook-chauffeur, was about to begin preparing supper. The girl got up to leave, and we walked her to her car, and came back to the swimming pool, jubilant.

> I remember weeping, briefly, more in helpless rage than in sorrow. . . . But I really don't remember that evening at all.

The phone had been brought out to the pool, and now it rang. Billy was on the other side of the pool, doing what I took to be African improvisations to the sound of Aretha Franklin. And I picked up the phone.

It was David Moses [an author and close friend of Baldwin's]. It took awhile before the sound of his voice— I don't mean the *sound* of his voice, something *in* his voice—got through to me.

He said, "Jimmy—? Martin's just been shot," and I don't think I said anything, or felt anything. I'm not sure I knew who *Martin* was. Yet, though I know—or I think— the record player was still playing, silence fell. David said, "He's not dead yet"—*then* I knew who Martin was—"but it's a head wound—so—"

I don't remember what I said; obviously, I must have said something. Billy and Walter were watching me. I told them what David had said.

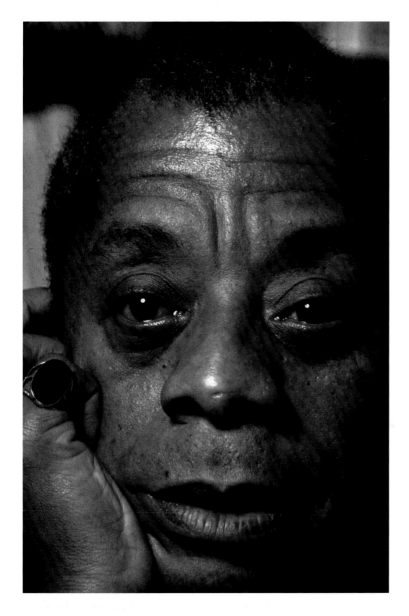

News of King's death overshadowed author James Baldwin's memories of the night of April 4, 1968. **(Time & Life Pictures/Getty Images.)**

I hardly remember the rest of that evening at all, it's retired into some deep cavern in my mind. We must have turned on the television set, if we had one, I don't remember. But we must have had one. I remember weeping, briefly, more in helpless rage than in sorrow, and Billy trying to comfort me. But I really don't remember that evening at all. Later, Walter told me that a car had prowled around the house all night.

Medgar Evers

The very last time I saw Medgar Evers [a civil rights worker assassinated in 1963], he stopped at his house on the way to the airport so I could autograph my books for him and his wife and children. I remember Myrilie Evers standing outside, smiling, and we waved, and Medgar drove to the airport and put me on the plane. He grinned that kind of country boy preacher's grin of his, and we said we'd see each other soon.

Months later, I was in Puerto Rico, working on the last act of my play. My host and hostess, and my friend, Lucien, and I, had spent a day or so wandering around the island, and now we were driving home. It was a wonderful, bright, sunny day, the top to the car was down, we were laughing and talking, and the radio was playing. Then the music stopped, and a voice announced that Medgar Evers had been shot to death in the carport of his home, and his wife and children had seen that big man fall.

> I said something like, 'That's a friend of mine—!'

No, I can't describe it. I've thought of it often, or been haunted by it often. I said something like, "That's a friend of mine—!" but no one in the car really knew who he was, or what he had meant to me, and to so many people. For some reason, I didn't see him: I saw Myrilie, and the children. They were quite small children. The blue sky seemed to descend like a blanket, and the speed of the car, the wind against my face, seemed stifling, as though the elements were determined to stuff something down my throat, to fill me with something I could never contain. And I couldn't say anything, I couldn't cry; I just remembered his face, a bright, blunt, handsome face, and his weariness, which he wore like his skin, and the way he said *ro-aad* for road, and his telling me how the tatters of clothes from a lynched body hung, flapping, in the tree for days, and how he had to pass that tree every day. Medgar. Gone.

The Funeral

I went to Atlanta alone, I do not remember why. I wore the suit I had bought for my Carnegie Hall appearance with Martin [in New York City, where Baldwin and King had been scheduled to speak together]. I seem to have had the foresight to have reserved a hotel room, for I vaguely remember stopping in the hotel and talking to two or three preacher type looking men, and we started off in the direction of the church. We had not got far before it became very clear that we would never get anywhere near it. We went in this direction and then in that direction, but the press of people choked us off. I began to wish that I had not come incognito, and alone, for now that I was in Atlanta, I wanted to get inside the church. I lost my companions and sort of squeezed my way, inch by inch, closer to the church. But, directly between me and the church, there was an impassable wall of people. Squeezing my way up to this point, I had considered myself lucky to be small; but now my size worked against me, for, though there were people on the church steps who knew me, whom I knew, they could not possibly see me, and I could not shout. I squeezed a few more inches and asked a very big man ahead of me please to let me through. He moved and said, "Yeah, let me see you get through this big Cadillac." It was true—there it was, smack in front of me, big as a house. I saw Jim Brown [a football player and actor] at a distance, but he didn't see me. I leaned up on the car, making frantic signals,

> I did not want to weep for Martin; tears seemed futile. But I may also have been afraid . . . that if I began to weep, I would not be able to stop.

and, finally, someone on the church steps did see me and came to the car and sort of lifted me over. I talked to Jim Brown for a minute, and then somebody led me into the church and I sat down.

The church was packed, of course, incredibly so. Far in the front, I saw [singer] Harry Belafonte sitting next to [King's widow] Coretta King. I had interviewed Coretta years ago, when I was doing a profile on her husband. We had got on very well; she had a nice, free laugh. Ralph David Abernathy [a civil rights worker and King's close associate] sat in the pulpit. I remembered him from years ago, sitting in his shirtsleeves in the house in Montgomery, big, black, and cheerful, pouring some cool soft drink, and, later, getting me settled in a nearby hotel. In the pew directly before me sat [acclaimed entertainers] Marlon Brando, Sammy Davis, Eartha Kitt—covered in black, looking like a lost ten-year-old girl—and Sidney Poitier, in the same pew, or nearby. Marlon saw me and nodded. The atmosphere was black, with a tension indescribable—as though something, perhaps the heavens, perhaps the earth, might crack. Everyone sat very still.

> I think I have never seen a face quite like that face that afternoon. She was singing it for Martin, and for us.

The actual service sort of washed over me, in waves. It wasn't that it seemed unreal; it was the most real church service I've ever sat through in my life, or ever hope to sit through; but I have a childhood hangover thing about not weeping in public, and I was concentrating on holding myself together. I did not want to weep for Martin; tears seemed futile. But I may also have been afraid, and I could not have been the only one, that if I began to weep, I would not be able to stop. There was more than enough to weep for, if one was to weep—so many of us, cut down, so soon. Medgar, Malcolm, Martin: and their widows, and their children. Reverend Ralph David Abernathy asked a certain sister to sing a song which Martin had loved—"once more," said Ralph David, "for Martin and for me," and he sat down.

My Heavenly Father Watches over Me

The long, dark sister, whose name I do not remember, rose, very beautiful in her robes, and in her covered grief, and began to sing. It was a song I knew: "My Heavenly Father Watches Over Me." The song rang out as it might have over dark fields, long ago; she was singing of a covenant a people had made, long ago, with life, and with that larger life which ends in revelation and which moves in love.

He guides the eagle through the pathless air.

She stood there, and she sang it. How she bore it, I do not know; I think I have never seen a face quite like that face that afternoon. She was singing it for Martin, and for us.

And surely, He
Remembers me.
My heavenly Father watches over me.

At last, we were standing, and filing out, to walk behind Martin, home. I found myself between Marlon and Sammy.

I had not been aware of the people when I had been pressing past them to get to the church. But, now, as we came out, and I looked up the road, I saw them. They were all along the road, on either side, they were on all the roofs, on either side. Every inch of ground, as far as the eye could see, was black with black people, and they stood in silence. It was the silence that undid me. I started to cry, and I stumbled, and Sammy grabbed my arm. We started to walk.

Witnesses Recall the Riots in Washington, D.C., Following King's Death

Virginia Ali and George Pelecanos, interviewed by Denise Kersten Wills

In the following viewpoint, Denise Kersten Wills, a staff writer for the *Washingtonian*, interviews two witnesses to the riots in Washington, D.C., following Martin Luther King's assassination. At the time of the rioting, George Pelecanos—now a writer and television producer—was eleven years old, and Virginia Ali owned a restaurant. On the fortieth anniversary of the riots, the two discuss the violence, anger, grief, and hope for change that both inspired and emerged from the rioting.

SOURCE. Virginia Ali and George Pelecanos, interviewed by Denise Kersten Wills, "People Were Out of Control: Remembering the 1968 Riots," *Washingtonian*, April 1, 2008. Reproduced by permission of the author.

"I don't like to predict violence," Martin Luther King Jr. told an audience at Washington National Cathedral on March 31, 1968. The mostly white crowd of 4,000 packed the cathedral and spilled onto the lawn.

"But if nothing is done between now and June to raise ghetto hope," King continued, "I feel this summer will not only be as bad but worse than last year."

Assassination and Anger

Angered by poor living conditions, unemployment, and discrimination, African-Americans in 1967 rioted in cities across the country. Twenty-seven people died in Newark, 43 in Detroit.

Four days after his sermon at the cathedral—on Thursday, April 4—King was assassinated in Memphis.

At the busy intersection of 14th and U streets in Northwest DC—the heart of the District's black community—the news arrived on teenagers' transistor radios. People began to gather at the intersection, which was near the Washington office of King's Southern Christian Leadership Conference.

Stokely Carmichael—a Howard University graduate who would later become a nationally known Black Panther—led a group of young men into nearby businesses, demanding they shut down as they had when President [John F.] Kennedy was killed in 1963. Carmichael urged people to remain calm, but the crowd grew.

Rioters, many of them teenagers, smashed windows, looted stores, and started fires. They tossed Molotov cocktails into buildings and threw bottles, bricks, and rocks at firefighters who tried to put out the blazes. The mood was part anger, part exhilaration.

> Rioters, many of them teenagers, smashed windows, looted stores, and started fires. . . . The mood was part anger, part exhilaration.

> One of the things that people don't realize or that they misremember is that rioting is a lot of fun.

Eleven-year-old George Pelecanos happened upon King's Washington National Cathedral sermon while in DC with his parents that day. As he roamed the crowd at the cathedral, he wondered what was holding the adults' attention. Days later, he could see the smoke over the District from his home in Silver Spring.

In 2004, Pelecanos revisited 1968 in his twelfth novel, *Hard Revolution*, a story that reaches its climax amid the riots. For research, he interviewed police officers, National Guard members, business owners, rioters, and other witnesses.

Virginia Ali and her husband, Ben, opened Ben's Chili Bowl in 1958 on U Street near the theaters and jazz clubs that had made the neighborhood famous as "black Broadway." The riots began just one block away, with a brick thrown through the window of the Peoples Drug at 14th and U [streets]. The Alis kept the restaurant open through it all; theirs was one of few businesses that went untouched.

Reflections on the Riot

On the 40th anniversary of the riots, we asked Pelecanos and Ali to reflect on the rioting and its aftermath.

Martin Luther King died at 8 pm on April 4. By 10, the crowd along 14th Street had turned violent. Off-duty police were called in, and a force of 2,500 law-enforcement officers managed to reestablish order in the early morning. By then, 150 stores had been looted and 200 people arrested.

Virginia Ali: I remember the sadness more than anything else. The radio stations were playing hymns, and people were coming in crying.

People were out of control with anger and sadness and frustration. They broke into the liquor store across the street and were coming out with bottles of Courvoisier. They had no money, these youngsters. They were coming into the Chili Bowl saying, "Could you just give us a chili dog or a chili half smoke? We'll give you this."

George Pelecanos: One of the things that people don't realize or that they misremember is that rioting is a lot of fun. It wasn't all political. It was kids having fun: "Let's go down there and get something. Let's throw rocks through the windows and see what we can get.

Ali: It had happened in so many other cities. We thought for a while Washington might be immune. We've got the government here, and we've got quite a few jobs. But still there was that fear.

Somehow I was not afraid in the restaurant. There's something about this place that makes me feel safer here than at home.

On Friday, April 5, rioting spread to other sections of the District, especially Seventh Street in Northwest, H Street in Northeast, and parts of Anacostia. Federal troops and the National Guard were called in; they would number more than 23,600. Mayor Walter Washington ordered a 5:30 pm curfew.

Pelecanos: The biggest mistake on the administrative side was not closing the schools and the government on Friday. Fourteenth Street had burned down, and officials thought it was over. But overnight, people all over the city had started talking about what was going to happen the next day. It got around by what they call the ghetto telegraph—the stoop, the barbershop, telephones.

Very early in the morning, the teachers and school administrators started freaking out because the students were out of control—they just started to walk out. Even down on the F Street corridor, which everyone thought was protected, you had kids running through Woodward & Lothrop screaming at people.

All of a sudden, panic started. People realized: This isn't over. It's just beginning, and we have got to get out of here.

Ali: I remember driving home and seeing droves of kids crossing over 13th Street near Cardozo High School. A group of them came and banged on our car. We had guests from Trinidad, and they were terrified. I was more intimidated by the National Guard standing outside our door with a big weapon than by the gangs.

We put a sign in the window that said "soul brother." We were not the only ones who did that. It was supposed to identify an African-American business. Some of them were saved, but some were burned.

We were the only place that remained open during the curfew. Stokely Carmichael told me, "You are going to stay open. We need a place to meet to see what we can do to quell the violence. City officials and police officers will be coming here."

I said, "There's a curfew. How are my employees going to get through?" Next thing I know, we've got passes for the employees.

A Miracle No One Was Shot

The riots continued on Saturday. Despite the chaos and demands from federal officials, Mayor Washington refused to order police to shoot rioters.

Ali: Near the front door, we had a cabinet with the electrical system. I opened it to turn on the lights in the evening, and tear gas came into my face. It must have come into the restaurant at some point and gotten trapped in the cabinet. It was stinging, and I was blinded.

I have relatives who lived way up past Park Road, about a mile from U Street; it was a nice area in those days. They said, "These people are moving uptown with their rioting and their burnings. I'm leaving town."

People felt close to the riots because of television. You're looking at it firsthand. Never mind that you live on Blagden Avenue and this is U Street—it's still Washington.

Pelecanos: I've met National Guard guys who have told me how incredibly scared they were. They had chicken wire on the fire trucks because they were being pelted with bottles and rocks while trying to get to the fires.

I've talked to police who are bitter because they couldn't use their weapons. I've also talked to police who are thankful they couldn't use their weapons because they would have killed somebody and they would not want to live with that.

Mayor Washington probably saved hundreds of lives. Most of the people who died got trapped in burning buildings. It's a miracle that nobody was shot on H Street or 7th Street or 14th Street. It's just a flat-out miracle.

> The people who lost the most were the people who lived in those neighborhoods.

The city smoldered on Sunday, but the worst was over. More than 800 fires had been started. Twelve people were dead and more than 1,000 injured. Rubble and charred buildings filled what had been vibrant neighborhoods—some are only now coming back to life.

Pelecanos: The people who lost the most were the people who lived in those neighborhoods. H Street was black Washington's shopping corridor. You had Sears, Morton's, Woolworth, and they employed thousands of black Washingtonians. All those jobs were gone, and people had no place to shop.

It virtually ended the downtown shopping experience. Nobody went downtown anymore. They were afraid.

Ali: Even my friends would say, "I want six chili dogs, but could someone bring them out to the car?"

Middle-class African-Americans had slowly started moving away with integration because the opportunity was there. You could move uptown and have a bigger yard, maybe a better school. Now people were afraid. Those who could afford to move away decided to.

This community had been so grand at one time, even though it was segregated. It was a community where everybody looked out for everybody else. If we were closed on Christmas Day, someone would call and say, "There's a truck parked in front of your place. Is somebody supposed to be there?" That's one of the things we lost.

> They needed to be shocked a little bit . . . to understand that nobody was going to wait another 25 years to get equality.

After the riots, you're seeing all these new people in the community. The slogans were "Black is beautiful" and "Power to the people." You had the new Afro, the big hairdo. Some people, particularly the older people, used to see that as a militant thing, which it really wasn't.

There were many boarded-up buildings, which made the neighborhood susceptible to drugs. In the 1980s, heroin addicts were on the corner by the hundreds.

No More Waiting

Pelecanos: To my young eye, the people had changed. They were standing taller, even wearing brighter clothing. I distinctly remember these big earrings with silhouettes of women with Afros that said black is beautiful.

This was still a south-of-the-Mason-Dixon-line city, but there was a different vibe. The riots made white people afraid, and through that fear they said to themselves, "Yes, things do have to change." They needed to be shocked a little bit. They needed to understand that nobody was going to wait another 25 years to get equality.

Ali: I don't think young people understand the struggle during that time. My kids say, "What do you mean you couldn't go downtown and eat in a restaurant? What do you mean you couldn't go to Garfinckels and try on a hat?" That's unreal to them.

When I look back at those riot tapes, I'm amazed we withstood it. It was a tragic time. We lost Dr. King, and I don't think we'll ever have a leader as passionate about nonviolence.

CHRONOLOGY

1955   December 1: Rosa Parks is arrested in Montgomery, Alabama, for refusing to give up her seat on a bus to a white person. African Americans boycott the city's buses.

December 5: Martin Luther King, Jr., joins the boycott and becomes its official spokesman.

1956   November 13: In response to the Montgomery bus boycott, the Supreme Court rules that bus segregation is illegal.

1957   King and other African American leaders and ministers form the Southern Christian Leadership Conference (SCLC), which aimed to fight segregation and obtain full civil rights for people of color.

1960   King becomes co-pastor with his father of the Ebenezer Baptist Church in Atlanta, Georgia.

1963   April 13: SCLC launches a campaign of nonviolent protest against segregation in Birmingham, Alabama.

April 16: After being arrested for participating in the SCLC protests in Birmingham, King writes his famous "Letter from a Birmingham Jail."

May 10: An agreement is announced to desegregate Birmingham.

August 28: The March on Washington, with 250,000

people in attendance, is the largest civil rights demonstration in history. King delivers his "I Have a Dream" speech.

November 22: President John F. Kennedy is assassinated in Dallas, Texas.

1964   July 2: King attends the signing ceremony of the Civil Rights Act of 1964, which had been pushed through Congress by President Lyndon Johnson.

December 10: King is awarded the Nobel Peace Prize.

1965   February 21: Malcolm X is assassinated in New York City.

March 21–25: King leads the third march from Selma to Montgomery, Alabama, as part of a series of marches in that state focusing national attention on the denial of voting rights to African Americans.

1967   April 4: King delivers the speech "Beyond Vietnam" in New York City, announcing his public opposition to the Vietnam War. The stance is extremely controversial.

November 27: King announces the Poor People's Campaign, which will focus on jobs and freedom for the poor regardless of race.

1968   March 28: King leads a march on behalf of sanitation workers in Memphis, Tennessee. The march turns violent, the first time this had happened in King's career.

April 3: King delivers his last speech, "I've Been to the Mountaintop."

April 4: King is shot and killed while standing on the

balcony of his motel in Memphis. King's death sparks riots in 130 cities, some of the largest occurring in Washington, D.C., Baltimore, Louisville, Kansas City, and Chicago.

April 9: King's funeral is held in Atlanta.

April 11: President Johnson signs the Open Housing Act, outlawing discrimination in housing.

May 12: The Poor People's Campaign begins its protests in Washington, D.C.

June: The Poor People's Campaign ends without achieving its goal of legislation to address economic injustices.

June 5: Robert F. Kennedy is assassinated in Los Angeles.

June 8: James Earl Ray, King's assassin, is captured by the Federal Bureau of Investigation in London, England, while trying to board a flight at Heathrow Airport.

1969 March 10: Ray pleads guilty to King's assassination. He is sentenced to ninety-nine years in prison.

March 13: Ray attempts to withdraw his guilty plea, claiming he did not assassinate King. Neither the plea nor the sentence is altered.

1976 The House Select Committee on Assassinations reinvestigates King's assassination. It finds that Ray was guilty, and may have conspired with his brothers. The committee concludes that the government was not involved in King's murder.

1986 Martin Luther King Jr. Day, a national holiday in honor of King, is established. It is observed on the third Monday of January each year, around the time of King's birthday.

1998   April 23: James Earl Ray dies in prison.

October 2: The King family files a wrongful death lawsuit against Loyd Jowers, the owner of a restaurant near where King was shot. Jowers claimed that others besides Ray, possibly including police, Mafia, and the federal government, were involved in the assassination.

1999   December 8: The jury in the wrongful death lawsuit filed by the King family finds against Loyd Jowers.

2000   June: A US Justice Department investigation concludes that no evidence supports Jowers' allegations of a conspiracy to kill Martin Luther King.

2006   Coretta Scott King, Martin Luther King's widow and an important civil rights figure, dies.

FOR FURTHER READING

Books

Janet L. Abu-Lughod, *Race, Space, and Riots in Chicago, New York, and Los Angeles.* New York: Oxford University Press, 2007.

Taylor Branch, *At Canaan's Edge: America in the King Years, 1965–1968.* New York: Simon & Schuster, 2007.

Taylor Branch, *Parting the Waters: America in the King Years, 1954–63.* New York: Simon & Schuster, 1989.

Taylor Branch, *Pillar of Fire: America in the King Years, 1963–65.* New York: Simon & Schuster, 1999.

Clayborne Carson and Kris Shepard, eds., *A Call to Conscience: The Landmark Speeches of Dr. Martin Luther King, Jr.* New York: Warner Books, 2001.

David Garrow, *Bearing the Cross: Martin Luther King, Jr. and the Southern Christian Leadership Conference.* New York: Harper Collins, 1986.

Michael K. Honey, *Going Down Jericho Road: The Memphis Strike, Martin Luther King's Last Campaign.* New York: W.W. Norton Inc., 2007.

Gerald D. McKnight, *The Last Crusade: Martin Luther King Jr., the FBI, and the Poor People's Campaign.* New York: Basic Books, 1998.

William Pepper, *An Act of State: The Execution of Martin Luther King* (Updated Edition). New York: Verso, 2008.

Gerald Posner, *Killing the Dream: James Earl Ray and the Assassination of Martin Luther King, Jr.* Orlando, FL: Harcourt Brace, 1998.

Hampton Sides, *Hellhound on His Trail: The Stalking of Martin Luther King, Jr. and the International Hunt for His Assassin.* New York: Random House, 2010.

Jules Witcover, *The Year the Dream Died: Revisiting 1968 in America*. New York: Warner Books, 1997.

Periodicals and Internet Sources

Daniel Akst, "Lingering Wounds," Boston Globe, January 18, 2009. www.boston.com/ae/books/articles/2009/01/18/lingering_wounds/.

Bryan Burrough, "Death of a Dream," *New York Times*, May 6, 2010. www.nytimes.com/2010/05/16/books/review/Burrough-t.html?_r=1&ref=martin_luther_jr_king.

Andrew Busch, "Remembering Which King?" *National Review Online*, January 12, 2007. http://article.nationalreview.com/303028/remembering-which-king/andrew-busch.

Earl Caldwell, "Martin Luther King Is Shot to Death in Memphis; White Suspect Is Hunted," *New York Times*, April 5, 1968.

Justin Ewers, "1968: A Spiral of Chaos and Death," *U.S. News & World Report*, January 17, 2008. www.usnews.com/news/politics/articles/2008/01/17/1968-a-spiral-of-chaos-and-death.html.

Darryl Fears, "Civil Rights Groups Seeing Gradual End of Their Era," *Washington Post*, April 5, 2008. www.washingtonpost.com/wp-dyn/content/article/2008/04/04/AR2008040403589.html.

David J. Garrow, "The FBI and Martin Luther King," *The Atlantic*, July/August 2002. www.theatlantic.com/magazine/archive/2002/07/the-fbi-and-martin-luther-king/2537/.

Fred P. Graham, "Suspect in Assassination of Dr. King Is Seized in London," *New York Times*, June 8, 1968. www.nytimes.com/learning/general/onthisday/big/0608.html.

Kathy Lohr, "Poor People's Campaign: A Dream Unfulfilled," NPR Online, June 19, 2008. www.npr.org/templates/story/story.php?storyId=91626373.

Kevin Merida, "The Other Side of the Mountaintop," *Washington Post*, April 4, 2008. www.washingtonpost.com/wp-dyn/content/article/2008/04/03/AR2008040304345.html.

Bill Moyers and Michael Winship, "Martin Luther King Jr.'s Economic Dream Still Unfulfilled, 42 Years Later," Salon, April 2, 2010. www.salon.com/news/opinion/feature/2010/04/02/martin_luther_king_assassination_anniversary_ext2010.

NPR Online, "Rev. Kyles Remember Martin Luther King, Jr." January 17, 2010. www.npr.org/templates/story/story.php?storyId=122670935.

Nicholas Schmidle, "The Stalker," *New Republic*, May 27, 2010. www.tnr.com/book/review/the-stalker.

Elana Schor, "Washington's Black Community Remembers 1968 Riots," *Guardian*, April 4, 2008. www.guardian.co.uk/world/2008/apr/04/1968theyearofrevolt.usa.

Paul Schwartzman and Robert E. Pierre, "From Ruins to Re-birth," *Washington Post*, April 6, 2008. www.washingtonpost.com/wp-dyn/content/article/2008/04/05/AR2008040501607.html.

Jonathan Steele, "King This Side of the Jordan," *Guardian*, April 6, 1968. www.guardian.co.uk/world/1968/apr/06/martin-luther-king-obituary-guardian-archive.

Time, "Investigations: The King Assassination," January 26, 1976. www.time.com/time/magazine/article/0,9171,913928,00.html?internalid=ACA.

Time, "Nation: King's Last March," April 19, 1968. www.time.com/time/magazine/article/0,9171,838205,00.html?internalid=ACA.

Time, "Nation: The Assassination," April 12, 1968. www.time.com/time/magazine/article/0,9171,838132,00.html?internalid=ACA.

Gary Younge, "America Lauds Martin Luther King, But Undermines His Legacy Every Day," *Guardian*, March 31, 2008. www.guardian.co.uk/commentisfree/2008/mar/31/usa.race.

Websites

The King Papers Project (http://mlk-kpp01.stanford.edu/index.php/kingpapers/index). A cooperative venture of the King Center, the King Estate, and Stanford University to publish a definitive fourteen-volume set of King's correspondence, sermons, and other papers. The website includes information about publications, news about ongoing projects, searchable access to thousands of King's papers, discussions of featured documents, and other resources.

The King Center (www.thekingcenter.org/Default.aspx). Website of the Martin Luther King Jr. Center for Nonviolent Social Change in Atlanta. It includes biographies and chronologies of the life of Dr. King and Coretta Scott King, discussions of the King holiday, a photo and video archive, and other resources.

The Seattle Times: Martin Luther King Jr. and the Civil Rights Movement (http://seattletimes.nwsource.com/special/mlk/). This online exhibit focuses on King as a civil rights leader. The website includes a biography; selections from King's speeches, sermons, and letters; photo galleries; links to Seattle Times articles; and study materials.

INDEX